SPEECHLESS

SPEECHLESS

SILENCING THE CHRISTIANS

Rev. Donald E. Wildmon

RICHARD VIGILANTE BOOKS

PUBLISHED BY RICHARD VIGILANTE BOOKS

Copyright © 2009 by Donald E. Wildmon

Foreword Copyright © 2009 by Ann Coulter

All Rights Reserved

www.richardvigilantebooks.com

RVB with the portrayal of a Labrador retriever in profile is a trademark

of Richard Vigilante Books

Book design by Charles Bork

Library of Congress Control Number: 2008942654

Applicable BISAC Codes:

REL084000   RELIGION / Religion, Politics & State

REL012110   RELIGION / Christian Life / Social Issues

REL108030   RELIGION / Christian Church / Leadership

POL004000   POLITICAL SCIENCE / Political Freedom & Security / Civil Rights

LAW018000   LAW / Constitutional

ISBN 978-0-9800763-3-2

PRINTED IN THE UNITED STATES OF AMERICA

10 9 8 7 6 5 4 3 2 1

First Edition

CONTENTS

FOREWORD

For as long as I can remember, liberals have been running around in a state of indignation, shouting that the government is being taken over by a dangerous band of religious fanatics who want to abolish the First Amendment, establish a national religion, force their bizarre sexual morality on children in public schools, rewrite the nation's laws to enforce their personal moral preferences, and punish anyone who dissents from their views.

Unfortunately, it's all true. That's precisely what liberals are trying to do.

As I explained in my book *Godless: The Church of Liberalism*, liberalism is a religion. It has its own cosmology, its own beliefs in the supernatural, its own churches, its own high priests, its own saints, its own total worldview, and its own explanation of the existence of the universe.

But for liberals, having their own religion is not enough. They want to impose it on the rest of us, and they have no conscience about how they do it. Conveniently, their religion teaches that there is no such thing as conscience. Whichever of their peculiar enthusiasms they are pushing at the moment, from Godless communism to compulsory pornographic instruction in public schools, to gay marriage, to "hate crime" and "antidiscrimination" laws that would make it a crime to express or act on Christian beliefs, it always comes from the same root. Liberals can justify anything because they believe in nothing. Specifically, they believe that man has no greater moral significance than an ape and that God is nothing more than a story some of the apes made up.

The fundamental liberal belief is a denial of the Christian faith in man's immortal soul. Their religion holds that there is nothing sacred about human consciousness. They deny the most important thing we know about ourselves: that we are moral beings in God's image.

Once the belief that man is a child of God is abandoned, then, as Sartre said, "Everything is permitted"—or at least everything that advances the liberal agenda. So it's no surprise that their version of the First Amendment protects "simulated child pornography," but allows them to pull the plug on a high school valedictorian's microphone when she mentions Jesus. (True story.)

Liberals' two favorite words are "tolerance" (good) and "judgmental" (bad). But in liberal theology these words mean something very different from what normal people mean by them. To most people, "tolerance" means limiting the power of government to the job of preserving ordered liberty so that people of different faiths or no faith at all can live together in peace. What liberals mean by tolerance is excluding Christianity (and Judaism) from any influence in public life. Since, for liberals public life is all of life, the ultimate logic is to make Christianity illegal. "Judgmental" means any objection to their plan. Under liberal theocracy we get a country in which taxpayers are forced to subsidize "artistic" exhibits of aborted fetuses, crucifixes in urine, and gay pornography. Meanwhile, among the things the Supreme Court has held "unconstitutional" are moments of silence in public schools, prayer in public schools, and displays of the Ten Commandments in public schools.

So is it that liberals have no conscience or just that they never listen to themselves talk? Liberals are constantly accusing Christians of intolerance, of refusing to see the other fellow's point of view, preachiness, and even of conducting a "war" against science of which we Christians are supposedly "afraid." But I almost never see these things in Christians, and I am always seeing them in liberals.

Take science. To be sure, Christians oppose Nazi-like experimentation on human embryos. So I guess you could say we oppose Nazi science. I have an idea—let's keep doing that.

Meanwhile liberals are terrified of, and hysterically lie about, any science that might challenge their worldview, especially their sexual worldview. So they lie about the AIDS virus, claiming, "Oh, AIDS doesn't discriminate between homosexual and heterosexuals." Well, it's been twenty years now. It looks like it does discriminate. Then we have the Harvard female professors of biology—fainting, nauseous, running from the room when then-president of Harvard Larry Summers suggests that perhaps it might be interesting to investigate whether men and women have different aptitudes in math and science. We have the lies about breast implants and the cancer clusters, although at least those lies were more about money (for trial lawyers) than sex. It's liberalism that is constantly opposing science because liberals can't stand it when science contradicts their fundamental moral principle, which is nondiscrimination (except against Christians).

Of course, another term for refusing to discriminate between things that are, you know, different, is refusing to acknowledge reality. Liberals live in a world in which even contemplating the idea that there are real and important differences between men and women makes them ill. No wonder they can't think of any objection to men marrying each other; the whole idea of an opposite sex frustrates them.

Liberals used to hate Christianity because it was the most powerful force in the world opposing communism. Now they hate Christianity because it is the most powerful force in the world opposing sexual depravity. In both cases their real enemy has been God.

That's why it drives them crazy that science keeps coming up with evidence disproving Darwin. I think if Darwin were alive today, he'd say, "Okay, you got me." Because Darwin, whatever his shortcomings, actually did what scientists are supposed to do and specified the evidence that would disprove his theory. He explained that his theory would be disproved if it could be shown that there is any biological form that could not have evolved by gradual steps: small mutations accumulating over time because each one was beneficial. At the time, neither Darwin nor anyone else had any idea of the inner workings of the cell at the molecular level. Now we do. And we know, as Michael Behe describes in his book *Darwin's Black Box: The Biochemical Challenge to Evolution*, the cell is more complicated than the most complex computer we have today. For that "computer" to be the result of Darwinian evolution, all the interlocking pieces would not only have had to randomly mutate into existence, but each mutation would have had to make the cell "more fit" *at the time the mutation took place*. Otherwise there would be no advantage to the mutation, and it would not survive and spread. But as Behe points out, the cell does not become more fit until all those mutations are working together in this interlocking machine. So the cell, a basic unit of life, could not have evolved gradually—thus it fails the standard Darwin himself proposed.

At this point Darwin is like Galileo or Hippocrates—a figure in history rather than in science. Meanwhile, scientists who take seriously the evidence that creation was guided by an intelligent designer are blacklisted and censured. Michael Behe was formally denounced by his entire department—for offering a scientific theory that contemplated the possibility of God. If he had not had tenure they certainly would have fired him.

If there is anything liberals accuse Christians of more often than being "intolerant" or "judgmental," it is not having an "open mind." But when the school board in Dover, Pennsylvania, wanted to include in the curriculum an innocuous, almost timid statement saying some scientists see evidence that evolution had help from an Intelligent Designer, and suggesting students might want to read up on the controversy *on their own time*, liberals sued. Winning the admiration of imbeciles at *Rolling Stone* magazine, a liberal federal judge ruled that suggesting that students think for themselves was unconstitutional.

Liberals can't give up on Darwin because without Darwin they have to confront God. Christians wouldn't be disturbed if evolution in some form were eventually supported by actual evidence. We believe the truth will make us free. But the idea of a God who made man in His image shatters the liberal worldview.

That's why taking over the pubic schools is so important to them. One thing I'll give liberals credit for is they've got a lot of energy. They will not give up. If they are not teaching "fisting" in public high schools, they are forcing third graders to read *Heather Has Two Mommies*. Just to hold the line at somewhere short of bestiality, normal people have to endure another endless debate about the latest liberal depravity, go to school board meetings for hours, organize their neighbors, and meet with teachers to simply get them to teach things like reading and math rather than issuing propaganda on the virtues of lesbian motherhood. I get exhausted even reading these stories.

Liberals are always preparing to open another front—while you sleep they're waiting, planning, and drafting lawsuits. Conservatives can never say, "We've won." Like terrorists, liberals practice "asymmetric warfare." A single terrorist slips through one security cordon and blows himself up in a kindergarten, and the terrorists have defeated thousands of soldiers and police and citizens trying to keep the peace. That's what liberals do to parents. They never, ever, ever give up.

One of the liberals' latest tactics, which Rev. Wildmon details, is the Employment Non-Discrimination Act, or ENDA. It's a new tactic, but an old liberal idea: liberals believe bigotry is rampant in America, and only government can protect us. The truth is that the government has always been the chief sponsor of bigotry. Jim Crow was a government program. As Thomas Sowell has pointed out, it was not the bus company that wanted to force Rosa Parks to the back of the bus. The bus company wanted customers. It was the government that said, "Blacks must sit in the back of the bus."

But now, once again, we are being told that unless the government decides who can be a Boy Scout leader, or who can lead the church choir, or to whom you can rent the extra room in your house, we are going to be consumed by hate. Because when liberals look at Christians they see—noxious bigots, you know—people who "cling bitterly to their religion and their guns."

Of course it won't be easy for liberals to convince Americans that Christians are dangerous lunatics inasmuch as the overwhelming majority of Americans are Christians. But the liberals' rallying cry is "separation of church and state," which means this: Christians, stay out of politics.

Well, we can't stay out of politics. This is our world we're fighting for, right now. Of course the government is not supposed to be religious. But the reason that Christians don't want the government to be religious—and the First Amendment was a Christian idea—is that we are religious. We want to limit the power of government, because given the chance, government will try to squeeze out any rival to its power—especially God.

Liberals want just the opposite. For them separation of church and state is a door that swings only one way. Every time the government expands into a new aspect of our life, suddenly we have to "separate out" religion. First they claim there is no place for religion in the public square, then they expand the public square to include everything.

Expanding the liberal state requires marginalizing Christians and religious Jews. Interestingly, liberals haven't objected to Muslims in the public square—at least not since 9/11. Perhaps the reason liberals are so protective of insane fundamentalist Islam is that they share the same theory of government.

Back in the days of the Prophet, when the Muslims conquered a new region, after the initial bloodbath, they did not force everyone to convert to Islam. Those who submitted to Muslim rule but did not convert were subjected to the law of dhimmitude. Christians and Jews were forbidden to preach, made subject to sharia law, and punished with special taxes and a host of legal disabilities intended to humiliate, impoverish, and marginalize them. That way, the Muslims could eliminate rival faiths over time without having to admit to violating the passage in the Koran that says, "There is no compulsion in religion."

See—liberals are not persecuting Christians. They are just imposing liberal sharia law, "Thou shalt rent thy spare bedroom to sodomites and fornicators; Thou shalt tithe to the government schools, even while paying to educate your own children in Christian schools or home schools; Thou shalt not counsel pregnant women that an abortion kills a child; Thou shalt not witness Christ in the public square." Meanwhile, liberals continue to expand that public square to include all of life. In the humiliate-and-impoverish department we have the spread of hate crimes legislation and so-called "antidiscrimination" in employment invoked only to punish Christians and Jews and to protect groups in favor with liberals—including their friends, the radical Islamists.

Of course there are violent crimes against homosexuals in this country—though not nearly as many as against black people and other minorities whom liberals have done so much to help. That's why gays should vote Republican. Conservatives want to prosecute violent criminals; liberals want to coddle them. Conservatives want to put muggers and murderers in prison; liberals want to put Christians in prison.

Essential to liberal dhimmitude is depriving Christians of the right to vote, or, as they call their total vote-suppression plan, "constitutional law." One day, liberals noticed that, as a practical matter, of the three branches of the federal government, the courts get the last word. So liberals decided they could use the courts to manufacture nonexistent rights rather than allowing Americans to vote (votes they lose). All of a sudden abortion is legal, any time, any place, under any circumstances, and Christians—or even heathens—never cast a vote. If Christians, indeed if 99 percent of all Americans agree that "simulated child pornography" should be outlawed, they lose without a vote being taken. They are gagged because liberal justices have announced that pornography is protected "speech." The greatest absurdity was probably when a liberal court discovered that the Massachusetts constitution, the one written by John Adams, creates a right for people of the same sex to get "married." I think that Adams, perhaps the most devout Christian of our Founding Fathers, would have been surprised to find that his constitution provided for that.

Actually Adams would have been more than surprised. He would have recognized tyranny. He would have understood those judges to be usurpers. Adams, and most of the rest of the Founding Fathers, would have refused to accept these judges as our dictators.

For forty years now, Christians have been meekly saying, "Oh gee, I guess we need to get some new judges and justices." That approach is not working very well. What really needs to happen is for some executive branch official, be it a governor or a president, to respond to one of these insane rulings from a court, a ruling that has no bearing on what is written in the document, by saying, "Thank you for your 'interpretation,' but since it is obviously insane, I'm going to ignore it."

Adams would do it; Washington would do it. And it would only need to happen one time for these judges to realize the game is over.

If there has been a turning point, I think it may turn out to be gay marriage. On the one hand, gay marriage is the ultimate weapon of liberal dhimmitude. If they can impose gay marriage on us by judicial fiat, their next move will be to make it a hate crime to not think *Will and Grace* is hilarious. Preferring not to celebrate sodomy will become the legal and moral equivalent of race discrimination. Anyone within the influence of those public institutions, any Christian teacher, any Christian civil servant, any Christian college professor, any Christian who does any business with government will have to proclaim sodomy a sacrament.

But with gay marriage they may have gone too far. I can't tell you how many people I meet at pro-marriage events or Christian events who say, "You know, I was never interested in politics. I'm a busy person. I'm going to Little League. I have a job. I have a family to support, but when they announced gay marriage, I got involved." And then they start to notice all the mischief liberals have been up to over the years. Until liberals grabbed their attention with gay marriage, they'd been happily occupied with their jobs, families, friends, hobbies, communities, and churches. Normal people isolate themselves from liberals as much as they can.

But that is becoming increasingly impossible. Liberals won't stop bothering everyone. They want total control of our lives.

That's why we need to fight back. We have to cut government and its false gods down to size, and we have to keep asserting our own religion just as loudly as they assert theirs. Well, maybe half as loudly. No one but a liberal could be that bossy. The number one tool they have against us is—us. It is our consent to their idea that we should keep our faith in the closet, especially on Election Day. Intimidating Christians into staying out of public life is the only way liberals can win.

The truth is Christianity is still a larger and somewhat more conventional religion than the godless religion of liberalism. Sure we are excluded from the mainstream media except when they want to do a story on how the "religious right" is a threat to human freedom as we know it or on the horrors of abstinence education. Yes, Hollywood portrays us as an obscure cult of skinheads. But it's whistling past the graveyard. We are a very powerful force. Look at the votes on gay marriage. Whenever people were allowed to vote—and by "people" I mean to exclude judges—gay marriage was overwhelmingly rejected. In the 2004 election, traditional marriage initiatives passed in state after state by far greater percentages than George Bush's margin of victory. In 2008, traditional marriage won big again, even in California, thanks to a great turnout by black voters.

It's the same with home schooling. Has anyone else noticed that even though liberals are constantly lecturing us that the key to education in America is small class size (translation: less work and more money for the clergy of the liberal religion), liberals hate home schoolers, who have the smallest class sizes around. But every time liberals try to crush home schooling, Christians roar like lions and liberal politicians run like rabbits.

Christians have long and rightly complained about the mainstream media. Don Wildmon was one of the first Christian leaders to do that in an organized, effective way. And it is still awful. But one thing has changed—the mainstream media is no longer mainstream. It actually shocks me how rapidly the evening news is losing viewers. The nightly audience for ABC and NBC news has dropped to about seven million each. Even the fake news on CBS is down to five million. So that means in our nation of 305 million, 19 million people are watching network news—and they're all in nursing homes. The "mainstream media" could more accurately be called "6.2 percent media."

We must keep reminding ourselves: they are not the culture; we are the culture. Hollywood proves this every time it puts out another movie bashing the troops or mocking Christ, and it grosses six dollars, while *The Passion of the Christ*, with the entire establishment media against it, is a blockbuster. Liberals are staying up nights, hatching new plans, but it is not working anymore, which may be why they are getting so crazy—I mean even crazier than usual. Evangelicals are building megachurches and filling them to capacity, and now the best of the Catholic churches are packed again. Look at books like Rick Warren's *The Purpose Driven Life: What on Earth Am I Here For?* topping the best seller lists. No, as much as they try, liberals just can't get Americans to abandon Christianity and sign up with the liberal religion. Liberals can never get to a Christian. That's why totalitarian movements always go after the family and after the church. (But on the bright side, the first thing they usually do is kill the journalists and intellectuals.)

One thing Christians need to know is how powerful grassroots activism is. Letters and phone calls to your congressmen and senators have an enormous effect. Remember, unlike judges, members of congress have to stand for re-election. When I was working for the Senate Judiciary Committee, there was one issue we got more mail on than anything else and that was the UN treaty on the rights of the child, which President Clinton was pushing. Every day we would get bales and bales of mail from voters livid with rage against the treaty. No one could figure out what had set off the Christians and conservatives. It turned out Phyllis Schlafly had penned one little column on it. People were alarmed and they started writing. With extra staffers needed to sort through the mail in every congressional office, there was just no chance that treaty was going anywhere.

Because we worship God and not the government, sometimes we're not as effective in getting our voices heard in the political debate. But I believe that the common sense of the majority of American people will prevail, as long as the people know what is going on.

Liberals only win on these issues when no one's looking. They're like roaches. They operate in the dark. Shine a light on them and they scatter.

Don Wildmon, a true American hero, has been shining that light for decades. From the very beginning, he saw the slippery slope that led us from Hugh Hefner to *Heather Has Two Mommies*.

Rev. Wildmon saw—earlier than anyone I can think of—that the sexual revolution and the secular assault on Christianity were one and the same thing. The pederasts and pornographers knew it. Their legal lackeys in the ACLU knew it. But Christians were slow to catch on, maybe because we believe in things like mercy and pity and forgiveness and hope.

Don Wildmon understood that evil follows the path of least resistance, that it will find its way to the weak points of a society, then wear away at them until resistance is not just futile, but unimaginable.

So read this book and then pass it on. Help shine the light. Don't be silenced.

Don't be *Speechless*.

Ann Coulter

CHAPTER ONE

Silence, Christians

They said it was offensive because it identified a particular religion. I really think it's free speech. We're Americans; we should be able to handle that.

—Brittany McComb, valedictorian,
Foothill High School, Henderson, Nevada

In 2006, Foothill High School in Henderson, Nevada, held its annual graduation ceremony, featuring remarks from three valedictorians. One of the selected speakers was Brittany McComb. During her four years at Foothill High, Brittany achieved a 4.7 grade point average, the highest of her class.

The school gave Brittany a set of guidelines to help her write her remarks. The written "suggestions" encouraged her to say things that came from her heart, to talk about things that "bind us together," and to "interject hope." She was also instructed to make it "more personal." Brittany took those instructions to heart and wrote a speech that met all the criteria.†

Brittany's speech titled "Filling the Void" described the emptiness she felt despite the accomplishments of her early high school years contrasted with the fulfillment she later felt when she became a Christian. Following school district policy requiring advance approval of such speeches, Brittany gave a copy of her speech to Roy Thompson, Foothill's assistant principal.

A week later, Thompson told Brittany that an attorney for the school district would review her speech. Usually when these speeches are vetted, school administrators are looking for obscene or offensive words.

After the school board attorney had reviewed Brittany's speech, she was summoned to a meeting with Thompson and the school's principal, Gretchen Crehan. During that meeting, a copy of her speech was returned to Brittany with substantial passages circled, annotated, and even crossed out. The edited portions constituted more than one-third of the entire speech. Handwritten notes described the offending passages as "Identifies a particular religion," "Deities," and "Proselytizing."

Brittany was told that she could not deliver the speech as written because of the religious references, which included three Bible passages, several mentions of "the Lord," and one reference to "Christ." The school board objected to the mention of a personal relationship with Jesus Christ as the catalyst for Brittany's high achievement.[†] She was told that she could mention God but not Jesus because Jesus identified a particular religion, Christianity.

Thompson and Crehan told Brittany to rewrite her speech following these rules and gave her the telephone number of the school board attorney if she had any questions.

When Brittany returned home, she told her parents what had happened. Brittany's mother, Constance, called the school board attorney three times; he never returned her calls. Brittany and her parents contacted Assistant Principal Thompson who told them that they would have to hire a lawyer to speak with the school board attorney. Brittany's father, Michael, hired a lawyer who wrote and called several times but never received any communication from either the school board or its attorney.

As graduation approached, Thompson began pressuring Brittany about her speech. Before the last day of classes, Thompson took Brittany aside and said he needed to know then what she planned to do. Brittany replied that she would let him know the next day before school. Thompson said, "Fine."

When Brittany had first written her speech, she was hoping to tell the audience the secret to her success, just as the guidelines specified: "Tell your classmates what made you successful as valedictorian." Her honest answer to that question was that Christ was a big part of her success and happiness.

Brittany believed that giving the speech as the school administrators had censored it would be dishonest and a violation of her principles. Brittany prayed about it. She remembered that Jesus stood up and spoke the truth. So she decided to give the speech as she had originally written it.

Brittany was not secretive or dishonest. She told Thompson of her intentions. That same day, Brittany's mother called the school board attorney a fourth time. She spoke to a school secretary who said that she hadn't seen any of the McCombs' prior messages. The secretary told Constance that she would talk to the attorney and call her back in five minutes. The call never came.

On June 15, Brittany and her parents went to the graduation ceremony together. Just before the ceremony began, Christopher Sefcheck, a faculty member, told Brittany he would be controlling the onstage microphone during the ceremony. He said he had the edited version of Brittany's speech and that he had been instructed to cut off the microphone if anyone deviated from the approved speeches.

When her turn came, Brittany rose from her seat on the stage and took her place before the microphone to deliver her speech in front of her family, four hundred of her fellow students, their families, and the school staff. Although she had the censored speech in her hands, Brittany had memorized the original version, which she planned to deliver. She began speaking. But when she mentioned God's love and giving up His only Son, the microphone was abruptly cut off. The audience reacted with a chorus of boos. Brittany remembers, "It was a surreal moment. I wasn't angry. I wasn't necessarily sad." The audience's support of her "was affirming." More important, before she had ever arrived at school that day, she "already knew that I had made the right decision."

Crehan then approached Brittany and told her that the microphone would not be turned back on. Brittany's speech was over. The crowd was incensed. Videotapes reveal the crowd chanting, "Let her speak. Let her speak."

Brittany had wanted to tell her classmates how the void of her early years had been filled with a sense of purpose through the love of God and her faith in Jesus Christ. But she was prevented from doing so.

Here is the text of her speech in its entirety. Ask yourself whether this should be forbidden speech in America:

"Filling the Void"

"Do you remember those blocks? The ones that fit into cutouts and teach you all the different shapes? The ones you played with before kindergarten, during the good old, no-grades, no-pressure, preschool days? I find it funny how easily amused we are as children. Many of us would have sat on the story rug for hours with those blocks, trying to fit the circle into the square cut-out. Thank the Lord for patient teachers.

"As one of the valedictorians for our senior class, many might assume I caught on to which blocks fit into which cut-outs quickly. But, to be honest, it took me a while. Up until my freshman year in high school, I continually filled certain voids with shapes that proved often peculiar and always too small.

"The main shape I wrestled with over the years remains my accomplishments. They defined my self-worth at a young age. I swam competitively throughout junior high and high school. If I took third in a competition rather than first, I found I missed the mark; I failed.

"But strangely enough, if I took first, I belittled my success, and even first place left me feeling empty. Either way, the shape entitled "accomplishments" proved too small to fill the void, constantly reminding me living means something more. Something more than me and what I do with my life, something more than my friends and what they do with their own lives.

"The summer after my freshman year, I quit swimming. I quit trying to fill the huge void in my soul with the meager accomplishments I obtained there. After quitting, this amazing sense of peace rushed over me and I noticed, after fifteen years of sitting on the story-time rug, this teacher standing above me, trying to help me: God. I disregarded His guidance for years, and all the while, He sought to show me what shape fits into the cut-out in my soul.

"This hole gapes as a wide-open trench when filled with swimming, with friends, with family, with dating, with shopping, with partying, with drinking, with anything but God. But His love fits. His love is "that something more" we all desire. It's unprejudiced, it's merciful, it's free, it's real, it's huge, and it's everlasting [audience cheering and applause]. God's love is so great that he gave His only Son up . . . [microphone goes dead here] to an excruciating death on a cross so His blood would cover all our shortcomings and provide for us a way to heaven in accepting this grace.

"This is why Christ died. John 10:10 says He died so we no longer have to reach in vain for the magnificence of the stars and find we always fall short, so we can have life—and life to the fullest. I now desire not my own will, but the will of God for my life—however crazy and extravagant, or seemingly mundane and uneventful that might be. Strangely enough, surrendering my own will for the will of God, giving up control, gave me peace, gave me a calm I can't even begin to express with words.

"Four years ago, recognition as one of the valedictorians for our senior class would have been just another attempt to fit the circle into the square cut-out. But because my heart is so full of God's love, the honor of speaking today is just that: an honor. Without it, I would feel just as full and purposeful as I do at this moment.

"And I can guarantee, 100 percent, no doubt in my mind, that as I choose to fill myself with God's love rather than with the things society tells me will satisfy me, I will find success; I will always retain a sense of self-worth. I will thrive whether I attend a prestigious university next fall and become a successful career woman or begin a life-long manager position at McDonald's.

"Because the fact of the matter remains, man possesses an innate desire to take part in something greater than himself. That something is God's plan. And God's plan for each of our lives may not leave us with an impressive and extensive résumé; but if we pursue His plan, He promises to fill us. Jeremiah 29:11 says, 'For I know the plans I have for you,' declares the Lord, 'plans to prosper you and not to harm you, plans to give you a hope and a future.'

"Trust me, this block fits."

Following the ceremony, Brittany got nothing but support from her fellow students. "All of my classmates came up to me and were so happy," Brittany said. "They told me they loved me, and I said God's awesome because I couldn't have done it without Him."

Encouraged by this reaction and convinced that she had done the right thing, Brittany contacted the Rutherford Institute, a nonprofit legal organization that specializes in defending religious liberty. The Rutherford Institute filed a First Amendment lawsuit on her behalf. Brittany's case made national news, and she appeared on *Hannity & Colmes, The Today Show*, and other television programs.

Brittany won the first round of the legal battle. But the school district, represented by the American Civil Liberties Union, has filed federal motions to dismiss the case. The judge, who seems to believe there is a serious constitutional principle involved, has denied these motions for dismissal, and Brittany's case will likely go to trial. There is a good chance she will win.

So what's the problem, you might ask? If Brittany wins her case an important principle will be established, all will be well, this will never happen again in America, and the story will have a happy ending, right?

Unfortunately, no. For as shocking as Brittany's case is, it is only one small incident in a much larger and more frightening story. It is a story I would find hard to believe myself if I had not been a personal witness to its unfolding for decades now. The silencing of Brittany was a small skirmish in a massive and growing campaign being waged by some of the most powerful interest groups in America to silence Christians, to keep us from witnessing to our faith or from speaking our consciences.

I say that this is a campaign by interest groups because these groups have very real interests, very real desires at stake, desires that, as usual, come down to sex, money, and power. Up until now, most Christians have not been aware that this battle has been going on. Most Christians don't realize that our adversaries see us as obstacles to their ambition, greed, and lust and are convinced that they must get us out of the way. But our adversaries know it. They have known it for decades. And Christians winning one court case, or a dozen court cases—as important as that is—will not stop or even seriously inconvenience the forces that want to render Christians speechless.

As I mentioned, this battle has been going on for more than a generation. But over the past few years it has accelerated and intensified. At one time, our opponents—a coalition of liberal secularists, homosexual activists, and a huge portion of corporate America that has been suborned by fear and greed—claimed that they were only seeking tolerance. Some of us never believed that. We always knew they wanted not tolerance but dominance, not acceptance under the rules but the power to rewrite the rules to eliminate any opposition or even any criticism. Most of them hid their goals at first, but no longer. Now it is out in the open, and we must open our eyes to see. But still, most Christians, like the "foolish virgins" in Jesus' parable, are asleep and unprepared.

Brittany had her microphone cut off for speaking her conscience. Soon Christians in this country may be going to jail for doing the same. Some already have.

Across the country, students are being told they can't make any reference to God in assignments or in speeches, even in classroom discussions. But it's not just happening in our public schools. Christians are being silenced all across America: in the political debate, the public square, the workplace, and even in the sanctuary of our own churches.

> In schools across the country, students are being told they can't make any reference to God in assignments or in speeches, even in classroom discussions. I find that amazing in light of the intellectual community's insistence that classrooms be environments where ideas could be expressed openly.
>
> Janet Parshall, from the TV series *Speechless*

The American Family Association and INSP-The Inspiration

Network recently produced a fourteen-part documentary series titled *Speechless*, hosted by Janet Parshall, one of our great Christian journalists and talk-show hosts. The series documented the silencing of Christians who dared to profess their faith, express their opinions, or even simply quote from the Bible. In this book I will tell some of those stories in even greater depth, as well as provide much new material that we were not able to fit into the documentaries. But even more important, we'll try to show who and what is driving this massive and coordinated campaign. If you have seen the series, you already know something about the threat to Christian faith and are curious to learn more. If you haven't seen the series, you may be shocked to learn how:

- A mother was not allowed to read her son's favorite Bible verse in kindergarten.
- Christians were arrested and threatened with prison terms for expressing their belief that homosexual behavior is immoral.
- Seventh-grade students were forced to follow Muslim rituals and recite Islamic prayers.
- The chapel in a veterans' hospital was stripped of all religious symbols, including the cross and the Bible.
- A church was told by the government that it must allow its property to be used for a lesbian "civil union" ceremony or lose its tax exemption for that property.
- "Diversity" and "antibullying" programs are being used to promote homosexuality in public schools.
- A man in Canada was charged with hate crimes because he wrote a letter to the editor of his local newspaper criticizing homosexuality.
- A group of municipal workers was told that saying the words "family values" created an offensive workplace environment.

- When Catholic Charities in Massachusetts, one of the largest adoption agencies in the state, refused to give babies to same-sex couples, the state forced it out of the adoption business.

- Employees of Fortune 500 companies are being fired for quoting the scriptures. Other employees are being told that displaying family pictures in their work cubicles could be offensive to homosexual employees.

- Proposed federal laws supposedly aimed at preventing employment discrimination against homosexuals (such discrimination is almost nonexistent today) could make increasing discrimination by Fortune 500 companies against Christians the law of the land and make it illegal for Christian churches to carry on their charitable works.

- Secularist liberals are pushing hard to reinstate the 1949 Fairness Doctrine, empowering the government to monitor all radio and television broadcasts for religious or political content, and giving the government power to censor or bankrupt Christian broadcasters.

- Under pressure from liberal secularists and homosexual lobbyists, the IRS is "cracking down" on Christian pastors who dare to criticize politicians who advocate homosexual propaganda in schools, abortion on demand, same-sex marriage, and other positions that fly in the face of Christian beliefs.

- If same-sex marriage becomes law all across America, homosexuality will be raised to the same legally protected status as race; any criticism of homosexuality would put employees, employers, pastors, and others at legal risk and expose them to cultural ostracism.

- Homosexuals will become part of an elite class of super-citizens whose moral views and interests will be actively sponsored by the state. Christians will be second-class citizens at best and their views will be censored, penalized, and even prosecuted.

These are powerful warning signs about how determined some of the most powerful forces in America are to rip out the Christian moral fiber of our culture.

But the big question that remains is, "Why?" Why should some of the most powerful and successful people in America turn against sacred American principles of freedom of speech and religion in order to silence Christians? Why would liberals especially, who once so prided themselves on their defense of free expression, give up what was once their most fundamental value? Why is it so important to these new liberals to drive Christians out of the public square and therefore underground? Why do Christian values make so many people see red? What explains the anger and the hatred directed at Christian pastors who speak out against public obscenity or for the unborn or who criticize corporations from Hollywood to Madison Avenue, from Las Vegas to Atlantic City, corporations that make hundreds of billions of dollars every year seducing Americans into crippling vices? How do you explain the venom directed at Christian politicians like Sarah Palin?

I think part of the explanation is very old—two thousand years old. The followers of Christ, even though few if any of us follow Him half as well as we should, have always been a scandal to the world and always will be.

Liberal secularists and their homosexual activist allies already constitute a political, economic, and cultural elite in our society. As studies show, compared to churchgoing Christians, secularists utterly dominate the media and cultural venues, the universities, and increasingly the top corporations. Why bother persecuting Christians?

Well, why did the Romans have to persecute the handful of Christians in their midst, mostly poor and powerless? Because, as the Roman culture became more and more depraved, as greed, adultery, and sexual perversion, materialism and the lust for power replaced the old Roman virtues of family and fidelity, self-sacrifice and public service, the Romans felt the Christians in their midst as a rebuke and an accusation. As Christians, however inadequately, tried to follow Christ's way, too many Romans concluded that the very presence of Christians constituted a criticism of their own behavior.

We can see this is true in the stories the Romans made up about Christians to justify their persecutions. Despite the poverty and powerlessness of the Christians, the Roman elite charged them with conspiring to subvert the government and imposing their morality on Rome. These mostly mild-mannered people were repeatedly reviled as a profound danger to the public order. Roman aristocrats of vast wealth and power, and even some emperors themselves, professed to be in real fear of this tiny Christian sect.

Obviously this fear was a fantasy—the Christians of Rome threatened no one. But although it was a fantasy, it was not a meaningless or random fantasy. Deep in their consciences, the Roman elite must have known they were marching toward sin and death. The emperor Augustus was profoundly worried that the Roman nobility was not reproducing itself. He saw that adultery, serial divorce, and sexual perversion were destroying the Roman family; too few of Rome's leading citizens were getting or staying married, and those who did marry had few children.

So the Romans knew something was wrong. Now I don't know about you, but few things can make me as angry as knowing deep in my heart that I am in the wrong, and then getting called on it. But do I get angry at myself? Of course not! I get angry at whoever showed me up, even if he or she didn't mean to. And that's what the Romans did. The example of Christian family life enraged the Roman elite, and in their anger they struck out at the Christians.

It may sound incredible, though I fear it won't be by the time you finish this book, but something very similar is happening in America today. For decades, a growing number of the American elite—the people who manage the media and mold the culture, run our great colleges and corporations, and train our lawyers and judges—has been gripped by a growing anger, now becoming a raging fury, against any person, group, church, or institution committed to Christian moral teachings.

Like the Romans, these people hear Christ's truth as an accusation. They even see Christ's love on the cross as their condemnation. And strangely enough, they see Christian families not as witnesses for Christ but as witnesses against them. I often think that if the anti-Christian elites only knew how hard we Christian families have to struggle to be true to Christ, and how often we fail, they would realize that we are in no position to accuse anyone. But then why were they so enraged by Gov. Sarah Palin, who so beautifully and generously gave us all an example of how Christian families struggle as much as any?

Of course the massive drive by the liberal elite to suppress Christianity (I mean those words exactly; like the Romans, they are not so much trying to eliminate Christianity as to drive it underground) isn't only about hidden guilt and anger. The coalition of liberal secularists and homosexual activists—let's call them "homosecularists" for short—have some very real goals that they know they can achieve only by driving Christians out of public life. Not surprisingly, those goals come down to sex, money, and power. And sex, as we are about to see, is the big one.

CHAPTER TWO

Why We Fight

Being queer means pushing the parameters of sex, sexuality, and family, and in the process, transforming the very fabric of society. . . . We must keep our eyes on the goal . . . of radically reordering society's views of reality.

—PAULA ETTELBRICK, EXECUTIVE DIRECTOR,
INTERNATIONAL GAY AND LESBIAN
HUMAN RIGHTS COMMISSION

We, as communists, used to debate people about the existence of God and after a while, I came to the conclusion that this was a waste of time. You aren't going to debate people away from the existence of God. But what we found was that if you get people involved in deviant sexual behavior, the whole idea of God just disappears automatically.

—WILLIAM REICH, AUSTRIAN-BORN PSYCHIATRIST (1933)

W hat does sex (not to mention money and power) have to do with whether Christians are allowed to witness their faith in public and in public life?

To begin to answer that question, let me share with you a very curious quotation from a prominent legal scholar named Chai R. Feldblum. Ms. Feldblum, a law professor at Georgetown University Law Center, is a lesbian and a passionate advocate of homosexual causes. She is also an honest and serious scholar. She concedes that secular liberals like her have increasingly turned away from their old commitment to freedom of speech and religion. But, she says, they had no choice. There is something the new generation of liberals has come to value more highly: what they call "sexual liberty." As a result, she says, when there is "a conflict between religious liberty and sexual liberty . . . in almost all cases sexual liberty should win."

You may ask, "Why should there be a conflict between sexual liberty and religious liberty? Why can't they go their own way and let us go ours, live and let live? Couldn't we just sit down with Ms. Feldblum and agree to disagree—do one of those "win-win" deals we always hear about in business?"

Unfortunately, "No." Because Ms. Feldblum is right. There is a conflict between what these new liberals call sexual liberty and our Christian beliefs. The liberals are not imagining it. Because of the way they define their sexual liberty, we really are in their way. And because the liberals saw this before we did, they have been working overtime to get us Christians out of the way. To really secure their sexual liberty, as they define it (not to mention the huge profits that come from catering to it), they must deny Christian morality any place in public life. They must push us underground.

One reason many Christians took no notice even while the culture war was erupting all around them is that the homosecularists always frame their first moves in the same way: they claim to be asking for nothing more than tolerance, which is the American way. But this claim is untrue, on two counts. They want a lot more than tolerance: they want our government and our culture to actively endorse, affirm, and support their worldview and their lifestyle. And to get that affirmation, they need us out of the way. They can't tolerate us; tolerance won't get them where they want to go.

Just look at the struggle waged over the First Amendment during the past several decades. Often this struggle is portrayed as some sort of "lawyers' technical argument" over the actual words and meaning of the amendment. The truth is nearly the opposite.

The homosecularists' real goal is to use the First Amendment as their weapon. Then, with the power of the government behind them, they can promote and enforce their values to ostracize Christians.

Here's what I mean. Pornography, which was pretty difficult to find in this country a couple of generations ago, is everywhere, thanks to secularist liberal lobbying and the courts. (I have been fighting it since Hugh Hefner's *Playboy*, which some people now consider to be relatively innocent. First lesson: don't let the camel get his nose in the tent.) Any serious attempt to legally restrict pornography—even just enough to protect minors—has been thwarted by the courts and the ever-vigilant American Civil Liberties Union and its allies. They say that protecting children is the parents' job and that it's "against the First Amendment" for government to help, as if parents alone could fight off the constant bombardment of smut being thrust at them all the time.

In other words: under the secularist liberal worldview the government *must* protect pornographers' freedom of expression but *must not* help parents protect their children from pornography. The secular liberals will say children are important. But when it's time to choose, they side with the pornographers.

A columnist at Townhall.com notes: "The federal judiciary is noticeably more open to obscenity than to religion. Laws barring public obscenity have been struck down on the grounds that passersby may 'effectively avoid further bombardment of their sensibilities simply by averting their eyes.'"

But if Christians have to avert their eyes, and shield their children's eyes, from pornography, obscenity, displays of homosexual behavior, and other things they find morally abhorrent (often funded by taxpayers), why can't liberals just plug their ears during Brittany McComb's speech? Isn't that the easy and obvious solution if free speech is their real concern? Wouldn't you think that any group so in favor of free speech that they refuse to protect children from pornography would be willing to let Brittany talk about Jesus?

> There's a door that swings one way in the wall of separation between church and state. How can we have art, subsidized at taxpayer expense, that's a crucifix in a vat of urine, but conversely, you can't have a nativity scene on a public square?
>
> Janet Parshall, from the TV series *Speechless*

The standard liberal line is that it is not their personal preference to silence Brittany any more than they have a personal preference for pornography. They have no choice they claim. They are simply doing what the Constitution requires. That claim is nonsense.

First, when push comes to shove, the American Civil Liberties Union and Americans United for Separation of Church and State and other anti-Christian groups lose a lot of religious liberty cases, especially in the higher courts. When the lawyers' technical arguments are made, Christians win cases like Brittany's (though not the pornography cases) at least as often as they lose. The ACLU and its liberal secularist allies go to court anyway because their real purpose, as we will see later, is not to win court cases or to "save the First Amendment" but to intimidate students, teachers, parents, and school districts so that there will never be a court case.

It's not surprising that we win a lot of the actual cases. The First Amendment was not written to protect multibillion-dollar pornography merchants *from the people*; it was written to *protect the people from government* trying to shut down political debate or from trying to control the churches.

Why did I choose pornography as an example? I didn't. They did. Most important First Amendment cases in recent decades centered around one of three issues: religious speech (as Brittany's did); political speech (usually where government is trying to use election finance laws to keep citizen groups from criticizing politicians); and obscenity. In those cases, Christians and other religious Americans consistently stood up for free speech and religion. The new liberals stood up for pornography not because of an abstract theory of the First Amendment but because, as Professor Feldblum says, they value sexual liberty more than religious liberty. In other words, it is more important to them to make sexual depravity seem OK than it is to protect children (or adults) from it.

(I mention adults because it is important to realize that in opposing pornography Christians are not trying so much to censor what "the other guy" can look at as to protect ourselves, especially we Christian men. It's not just "weirdo perverts" who get sucked into this stuff these days, but lots of Christian family men, too, who are overwhelmed by a temptation that is now everywhere. Pornography tempts most men, and it's "us," not "them," we're worried about.)

It is not the devotion of secular liberals to the First Amendment that compels them to defend pornography. Just the opposite. Their devotion to sexual liberty compels them to distort the First Amendment beyond recognition.

If you want to know what someone's values are, ask him what the First Amendment means. If he thinks it's meant to protect religious and political speech from the government, chances are he values religion and political liberty. If he thinks the purpose of the First Amendment is to undermine traditional moral teachings, then chances are . . . but you don't need me to tell you, they speak for themselves. In the words of Franklin E. Kameny, charter member of the Washington, DC, ACLU: "The First Amendment creates an inescapable moral relativism, societal and cultural, for our nation taken as a whole. For example, I view homosexual activity as not only not immoral, or sinful, or wrong, or undesirable, but as affirmatively moral, and virtuous, and right, and desirable."

The conflict between the sexual liberty of adults, as the new liberals have defined it, and the needs of children is especially grievous. This conflict was at the core of the sexual revolution. The struggle over easy, "no-fault" divorce was really a struggle over the needs of children versus the sexual liberty of the parent who wanted to leave the marriage, in some states on ninety days' notice! But with abortion the stakes were even higher: the sexual liberty of adults versus the lives of children. The sexual liberty of adults prevailed, and some forty-six million unborn children have been lost in the past thirty-five years.

The sexual liberals saw this conflict more clearly than we did, which is one reason they never talk about what Christians view as the real issue in abortion, the life of the baby. Of course discussing what abortion does to babies is not exactly a winning argument. But that is not the only reason secular liberals don't talk about babies. They talk about abortion in terms that matter to them. They see their right to abortion as a guarantee of their sexual freedom. And they truly believe that the real goal of the pro-life side is to control other people's sex lives.

Now you and I know that we don't even want to think about their sex lives, never mind control them. Still, it is true that restricting abortion would create pressure against promiscuity. And the new liberals see any such pressure as an outrageous violation of their sexual liberty. So naturally they are quite willing to silence pro-life Christians, for instance, by using federal antiracketeering laws (meant to go after organized crime) against Christians who protest outside abortion clinics.

The advocates of the sexual revolution constantly declaimed, "Sex is a private matter" by which they meant, "Christians, butt out. What we do in the privacy of our bedrooms is none of your business." But as honest secular liberals like Professor Feldblum concede, in many ways sex is a very public matter. Catastrophic divorce rates and fatherless children are a very public matter. Even further, the pornographic culture in which our marriages struggle and in which we try to raise our children is a very public matter. And as we are now being reminded, the very definition of marriage is a very public matter, which homosexual groups are trying to change radically, all the while claiming that all they really want is "tolerance."

Or at least that is what they used to claim, back when they were much weaker. In the past few years that has changed. Once again, I'll let them speak for themselves:

> We are no longer seeking just a right to privacy and a right to protection from wrong. We have a right—as heterosexuals have already—to see government and society affirm our lives.
>
> Jeffrey Levi
> National Gay and Lesbian Task Force

> People often get their views from religion, so we don't want the pulpit saying that being gay is wrong.
>
> Cathy Renna
> Renna Communications

> I believe gay love embodies the same moral goods as heterosexual love. My agenda would be for the rest of the country to believe those things as well.
>
> Chai R. Feldblum, "The Gay Agenda"

The sexual liberals, especially homosexual activists and their allies, crave public approval. And they are perfectly willing to use the power of government, and even persecute Christians, to get it.

Ironically, the homosexual lobby realizes that the best way to enforce its views on society is for homosexuals to be seen as "victims." That's why becoming official victims under various state and federal civil rights laws is a major part of its strategy. As a specially protected group, the lobby can, bit by bit, make it nearly impossible legally for any American to publicly advocate Christian moral teachings on sex.

Does that seem far-fetched? It's already happening and makes perfect sense under the law. Take laws against discrimination in employment or sexual harassment. Under current law, any corporation that endorses racist ideas or allows employees to make racist remarks at work or through office e-mail could be charged with trying to discourage blacks or other minority groups from working there—and justly so. Laws regarding sexual harassment make it clear that employers are not to allow "a hostile work environment" in which women might feel uncomfortable.

But when sexual liberals succeed in giving the practice of homosexuality the same specially protected legal status that the law gives to racial minorities or women, Christian employees who express support for Christian family values can be defined legally as bigots. Suddenly, a company can be sued for allowing its Christian employees to express their views. Naturally, many companies have instituted rules forbidding Christian speech, as we will see in chapter eight.

See how it works? The battle is not just about whether the ACLU or homosexuals win a lawsuit here or lose one there. It is about using the power of the government to leverage the whole culture *for* "sexual liberty" and *against* Christianity. As Janet Parshall, who hosts our TV series *Speechless* argues, "The homosexual lobby doesn't just want equal status with heterosexuals; they want special protection and special recognition."

Of course, this is a gradual process. The homosecularists use the law, for example, to insert homosexual propaganda into the schools or to drive Christian speech out of the schools, to nudge the culture a little in their direction. Then, as sexual liberty becomes more exalted in the culture and Christianity is thought to be something shameful to be practiced only in private, the homosecularists become more bold in their use of the law. If they can make it seem bigoted and intolerant for Christian ministers to preach that sodomy is a sin, then it becomes much easier to start taking away tax exemptions from churches. After all, who is going to support "tax subsidies," as liberals call any tax exemption they oppose, for bigots? Next thing, the IRS becomes the Inquisition.

When the homosexual movement first gained prominence, many of its demands seemed absurd. The 1972 Gay Rights Platform demanded that there be "federal encouragement and support for sex education courses, prepared and taught by gay women and men, presenting homosexuality as a valid, healthy preference and lifestyle and as a viable alternative to heterosexuality." Who in 1972 thought that could ever happen in America? Now it's happening in schools all over the country.

The secularists define "sexual liberty" as sexual, moral, and political affirmation. They have defined the battle as winner-take-all. It is they who have decided that their version of sexual liberty cannot coexist with real Christianity.

And right now the momentum is on the side of the homosecularist elite. They have succeeded in perverting the original meaning of our founding documents. Laws written to protect religious liberty are now used to suppress it. Christians are forced not only to accept homosexual behavior but also to actively support and encourage it, while the homosecularists deploy a strategy of legal maneuvers, political intimidation, and government-funded propaganda to discredit Christianity at every level of society.

This is a battle for the future. From the very beginning, homosecuralists have looked ahead while we Christians have told ourselves, "It can never happen here." For that reason our opponents' most important goal is to capture the schools and drive a wedge between Christian parents and their children ...

CHAPTER THREE

The Bully of the Schoolyard

The United States Constitution does not mention the right of parents to direct the upbringing of their children.

—THE AMERICAN CIVIL LIBERTIES UNION

There's no such thing as other people's children.

—SENATOR HILLARY RODHAM CLINTON

Instead of fearing being labeled pedophiles, we must proudly proclaim that sex is good, including children's sexuality. . . . Surrounded by pious moralists with deadening antisexual rules, we must be shameless rule breakers, demonstrating our allegiance to a higher concept of love. We must do it for the children's sake.

—THE GUIDE MAGAZINE

Perhaps the number one goal of the homosecularist elite is to use the schools to indoctrinate children into accepting homosexuality as perfectly normal and a morally acceptable choice. The homosecularists' challenge is that most Americans are Christians who would strongly object to such indoctrination. So the homosecularists need an excuse to slip homosexual propaganda into the schools in a way that disables parents' objections or makes parents seem mean and outdated for upholding Christian values.

The anti-Christians have tried a number of approaches, but their most effective approach yet is to push through an antibullying or "safe schools" curriculum that is really a cover for preaching homosexuality and condemning Christianity.

I have to admit that it's a brilliant ploy on their part. I know many parents who really are worried about bullying in the schools today. This is not surprising considering how many children are being raised today without any moral compass, or how few can even name the Ten Commandments. What happens is that the homosecularists exploit that concern and then twist it in three different ways.

First, they claim that by far the biggest bullying problem we have in the schools is bullying of homosexual students. Now this is something we could imagine being true. Many of us, unfortunately, can remember effeminate boys being picked on at school. So it begins with a plausible claim: bullying is a much bigger problem today, especially for homosexual students. As it turns out, this claim is untrue: most bullying has nothing to do with homosexuality. Still, it's plausible. It "sounds good."

Next, a curriculum that the homosecularists promised would be about school bullying ends up being mostly about homosexuality. Their justification for this is that children must not only be made familiar with homosexuality but also be told that it is perfectly normal, that it's OK. Only by teaching that homosexuality is OK can we stop this terrible (made up) bullying problem.

And then comes the real kicker. These curricula in the schools clearly state that any criticism of homosexuality, such as saying that sodomy is a sin, is bullying.

In other words, they get the public schools to explicitly teach that Christian moral teaching, or even students expressing Christian beliefs in conversations in the schoolyard, is a form of bullying, socially discredited, and officially prohibited by school regulations.

Can't happen in America? Can't happen in your town? Come on a little trip with me to Ashland, Kentucky, in Boyd County, USA.

Ashland is coal country. Nestled in the state's eastern corner on the borders of West Virginia and Ohio, its lifeblood is found in the mines beneath the ground and in the churches above. Big city problems don't invade this area very often. It's a tight-knit community where families raise their children on traditional values. So why do students and parents in Boyd County now find themselves fighting compulsory sexual-diversity training that promotes the homosexual lifestyle?†

True to form, the weapon that homosecularists used to push their way into Boyd County was a trumped-up charge of bullying. Here's what happened. With support from the ACLU, pro-homosexual activists in Boyd County formed a gay-straight alliance (GSA) club in the high school. Naturally enough, in a community like Ashland this was not a popular idea. Once the club was formed, nearly half of the school's students boycotted classes in protest. So the school board tried to find a way to keep the club out of the Boyd County public schools. They felt so strongly about the issue that they banned all extracurricular clubs. Then the ACLU took the school board to court and won. The school board was forced to allow the GSA to meet in the school. In the end, the club didn't amount to much; hardly anyone showed up at the meetings, and it was disbanded for lack of interest.

Now if that was the end of the story, I could see how fair-minded people might take either side of the argument. Maybe no matter how much pressure the school board was under from the students or the parents, they should have let the homosexual club meet in school in the first place. But that's not where it stopped. The court, at the ACLU's urging, used the excuse of the community not wanting a gay club in school to force the school to adopt an "antiharassment" training program, which of course turned out to be pro-homosexual and anti-Christian propaganda.

Even though the program was imposed as a result of the dispute over the Boyd County High School GSA club, parents say that they were never told that the ACLU program focused on homosexuality. As Mary Morrison, a Boyd County parent remembers it, parents were told, "This was an antiharassment, antibullying video. And they never brought up anything about homosexuality when they were discussing it. But then when you watched the video, the entire content of the video was on homosexuality." As Mary's husband, Tim, tells it, the whole point of the program was to teach acceptance of "the homosexual lifestyle.... And no matter what, you're to accept it."

A major part of the training was a film featuring a "compliance coordinator" discussing the issue of bullying with a group of students. The film begins by explaining how everyone is at risk of being bullied. But quickly the discussion focuses exclusively on sexual orientation and gender identity, as if this were the only reason kids get bullied. Then, the main point of the video is made:

"You're going to find people that you believe are absolutely wrong. You're going to think[, "W]hat are they thinking? That, that is so wrong; it['s] obvious to everybody[." B]ut not to them. But . . . just because you believe that does not give you permission to say anything about it."

What does that passage mean? Does it mean that students should not call other students names, which they certainly should not? Or does it mean that no student should ever say he thinks a particular type of behavior that another student may possibly practice is bad behavior? Does it mean that no student should say, "Lying is a sin" because it might seem like he's bullying students who lie?

The film avoids that extremely important question. But it makes very clear that the safest policy is to say absolutely nothing that could be construed as criticism of the homosexual lifestyle. As the compliance coordinator firmly states, "Our main goal today is to educate students that harassment and discrimination, either one of those, based on real or perceived sexual orientation or gender identity, will not be tolerated by your school system in any way."

By the time Tim and Mary Morrison's son T. J. was in his sophomore year, the atmosphere had gotten so oppressive that students couldn't say the word "gay," meaning homosexual, in school, though that is the word homosexual advocates claimed for themselves years ago. T. J. was told that if he used the word "gay" he would be suspended for five days. As T. J. commented, "They have a right to go out and say that they're gay and that gay is good and all this other stuff. I should have a right to say that I don't believe in it."

In such an atmosphere it is very clear that the safe thing for Christian students is never to say what they believe. Stay underground where the secularists want you. Predictably, even though many, perhaps most, of the students disagreed with the policy, they kept their thoughts to themselves.

The compliance coordinator who moderates the video tells students, "We would never try to influence [your religious beliefs]. They are very sacred and they should only be influenced by you and your parents and family."

In another curriculum dispute in Maryland, however, included in the curriculum was a handout that very directly criticized traditional Christian belief and taught as fact a bizarre reinterpretation of Christ's teaching. Titled "Myths and Facts," here is what that handout said about "Morality."

Myth: Homosexuality is a sin.

Facts: The Bible contains six passages which condemn homosexual behavior. The Bible also contains numerous passages condemning heterosexual behavior. Theologians and biblical scholars continue to differ on many biblical interpretations. They agree on one thing, however. Jesus said absolutely nothing at all about homosexuality. Among the many things deemed an abomination are adultery, incest, wearing clothing made from more than one kind of fiber, and eating shellfish, like shrimp and lobster.

Religion has often been misused to justify hatred and oppression. Less than a half a century ago, Baptist churches (among others) in this country defended racial segregation on the basis that it was condoned by the Bible.

Early Christians were not hostile to homosexuals. Intolerance became the dominant attitude only after the twelfth century. Today, many people no longer tolerate generalizations about homosexuality as pathology or sin. Few would condemn heterosexuality as immoral—despite the high incidence of rape, incest, child abuse, adultery, family violence, promiscuity, and venereal disease among heterosexuals. Fortunately, many within organized religions are beginning to address the homophobia of the church.

The homophobia of the church. But don't worry; the homosecularists would never, ever use a public school classroom to try to influence your children's religious beliefs.

The only bullies in the Boyd County case were the homosecularists who threatened a teenage boy with suspension from school if he used the word "gay." Tim and Mary were told that once their son stepped through the school door he belonged to the school district. Mary specifically asked, "You're telling me that

my child is no longer mine as long as he's on school property?"
And she was told, "That is correct."

Finally fed up, Tim and Mary with the help of the Alliance
Defense Fund filed a federal lawsuit to defend the First Amendment rights of T. J. and the other students critical of the program.
As Jordan Lorence, senior counsel of the Alliance Defense Fund
commented: "In a free society, people are going to hear things
they don't agree with. And if we can silence anyone who offends
us, there won't be much speech going on in America."

> In America, we have long protected the First Amendment
> right of free speech, even in cases where that speech is of-
> fensive. We may not agree with the protester's message,
> but it's not against the law. But that's changing.
>
> Janet Parshall, from the TV series *Speechless*

The initial court case resulted in a decision against the Boyd
County parents, but that ruling was appealed to the United States
Court of Appeals for the Sixth Circuit, which reversed the ruling
of the lower court and agreed that T. J. Morrison's right to free
speech had in fact been violated.

The case has been sent back to the lower court. The ACLU at
one point had a notice on their Web site stating, "If we can win
here, in this little town in Kentucky, we can win anywhere." † The
ACLU knew how important the Boyd County case was not only
strategically but also symbolically. By winning in a very traditional community, the ACLU could intimidate other communities without much effort.

Joining the ACLU in the nationwide campaign to promote
homosexuality in public schools nationwide is the Gay, Lesbian
and Straight Education Network (GLSEN). The ACLU published
a manual titled *Making Schools Safe*, which the organization is

trying to develop into a nationwide blueprint for homosexual indoctrination and censorship of Christians. So far, the ACLU is winning. At least eleven states (California, Connecticut, Iowa, Maine, Massachusetts, Maryland, Minnesota, New Jersey, Vermont, Washington, and Wisconsin) have passed legislation requiring "safe schools" programs with "sexual orientation" teaching included. Many others are debating it, while some states have introduced such a curriculum informally or only in certain districts. As in Boyd County, these programs are typically riddled with pro-homosexual propaganda and homosexual sex education. Children as young as preschoolers are being taught about homosexuality. The programs typically redefine a family as any combination of people bound together by ties of affection or intimacy. In the older grades, sodomy is often taught in very graphic terms.

Here are just a few examples of how these programs are promoting homosexuality and undermining parents' rights:

- The New Jersey Department of Education has promoted a half-hour documentary in schools throughout the state titled *That's a Family!* which shows children being raised by homosexual couples. In the town of Evesham, elementary schools began showing the film, which was screened at the Clinton White House in 2000, to third graders as part of their health curriculum.
- New Jersey State Health Education standards require that fourth-grade students learn about "different kinds of families," including same-sex families.
- Schools in Spurger, Texas; Bedford, Massachusetts; and Carrier Mills, Illinois, have conducted student "cross-dressing" events.
- In the theater presentation *Cootie Shots*, students are immunized against intolerance by listening to a cross-dressing boy sing "In Mommy's High Heels," based on lyrics by Paul Selig:

So let them jump and jeer and whirl
They are the swine, I am the pearl . . .
Let them laugh, let them scream,
They'll all be beheaded when I'm queen.
When I rule the world, when I rule the world,
In my Mommy's high heels.

- The film *It's Elementary: Talking About Gay Issues in School*, which has been shown in schools all across America, portrays a fifth-grade boy saying, "Some Christians believe that if you're gay, you'll go to hell, so they want to torture them and stuff." (But remember they respect your religion. They really do!)
- Homosexual "educational" programs have claimed that King David, Paul the Apostle, Abraham Lincoln, Alexander Hamilton, and other historical figures were homosexuals. Some have gone as far as arguing that Jesus Himself was homosexual.
- In 2006, a lesbian state senator from California proposed a law that would ban anything that "reflects adversely" on homosexuality in school textbooks.
- A lesson plan for kindergarteners in San Francisco called "My Family" describes homosexuals as "people of the same sex who have feelings for one another in a romantic way." And a family is a "unit of two or more persons, related either by birth or by choice, who may or may not live together, who try to meet each other's needs, and who share common goals and interests."
- The state of Maryland has put itself wholeheartedly behind the homosexual school agenda, and some professionals feel that the Maryland curriculum could become the model for promoting the homosexual lifestyle in public schools across the nation. The Maryland State Board of Education has

ruled that the rights of the state supersede the rights of parents in teaching children about homosexuality, proclaiming that parents' rights "must bend to the state's duty to educate its citizens."

Massachusetts has been such a "leader" in pushing homosexuality on schoolchildren that homosexual activists travel the country demonstrating how other states can be captured using similar tactics. In the Bay State:

- A school in Provincetown, Massachusetts, has begun teaching about homosexuality in preschool.
- A GLSEN (Gay, Lesbian and Straight Education Network) conference in Massachusetts in 2000 came to be known as "Fistgate" when students as young as fourteen were taught techniques of sadomasochistic homosexual sex in graphic detail.
- A health text given to high school freshmen in Silver Lake, Massachusetts, included this advice: "Testing your ability to function sexually and give pleasure to another person may be less threatening in your early teens with people of your own sex."
- The same text includes this gem: "You may come to the conclusion that growing up means rejecting the values of your parents."
- Students in Framingham, Massachusetts, were told to fill out a questionnaire that included these questions: "What do you think caused your heterosexuality? When did you first decide you were heterosexual? Is it possible that heterosexuality is a phase you will grow out of?"
- In Lexington, Massachusetts, a curriculum intended for kindergarten included a book titled *Who's in a Family?* by

Robert Skutch. It emphasizes the "positive aspects of different family structures," including same-sex parents. In the author's own words: "The whole purpose of the book was to get the subject [of same-sex parent households] out into the minds and the awareness of children before they are old enough to have been convinced that there's another way of looking at life."

Minnesota is jumping on the bandwagon too. Katherine Kersten, a brilliant columnist for Minneapolis' *Star Tribune* exposed the homsecularists' efforts there. Of course it was Kersten who got the hate mail. I was going to quote a paragraph or two from Kersten's column, but it's so good I have to quote the whole thing (by permission of the *Star Tribune*):

> The bully is the scourge of the elementary school playground. So who could object to a new antibullying curriculum scheduled to be tested in three Minneapolis elementary schools—Hale, Jefferson, and Park View—and adopted districtwide if successful?
>
> But what if that curriculum is really a disguise for a very different agenda brought to Minneapolis by the Human Rights Campaign, a Washington, DC-based gay and transgender advocacy group? What if its lessons have little to do with bullying and much to do with ensuring that kids as young as age five submit to HRC's orthodoxy on family structure, even if it differs from their own parents' view?
>
> What if students who dissent are subjected to teacher-directed peer pressure and negative evaluations?
>
> In other words, what if antibullying advocates themselves turn out to be the bullies?

Welcome to the "Welcoming Schools" curriculum.

In March, Minneapolis Superintendent Bill Green praised "Welcoming Schools" as "a tool to combat bullying, by focusing on diversity, gender stereotyping, and name-calling." But the curriculum's underlying social/political agenda leaps from every page.

"Welcoming Schools" has three sections. The first, on "family diversity," drums into kids the idea that "traditional families" are outdated. To emphasize this point, kids in grades three through five "act out" being members of nontraditional families, including same-gender-headed families.

K–third grade students study words like "lesbian" and "gay," while fourth- and fifth-graders learn "bisexual," "dyke," and "transgender."

In the curriculum's second section—"Looking at Gender Roles and Stereotyping"—children learn to "expand their notions of gender-appropriate behavior." They read books such as *Sissy Duckling*, which deals with "characters challenging gender norms," and *King and King*, in which a prince proposes to and marries another prince.

"Welcoming Schools" does not address bullying until its third and final section. It says relatively little about bullies' traditional targets—kids who are overweight, short, or the wrong skin color, for example—and places heavy emphasis on antigay name-calling.

To promote its agenda, "Welcoming Schools" employs classic indoctrination techniques.

Teachers begin lessons by questioning students to identify their current beliefs. Then they use group exercises, films, and books to convince the kids that any traditional attitudes they harbor about family structure and homosexuality are harmful "stereotypes." At the end of a lesson, teachers "evaluate" students to ensure that their views now pass official muster.

One fill-in-the-blank phrase that students are to complete during evaluation says it all: "I used to think, but now I know . . ."

The "Family Diversity Photo Puzzle," a typical lesson for grades one through three, exemplifies this approach.

In the exercise, the teacher instructs students to arrange photos of adults and children to create seven families. But the exercise is rigged, though children don't know it.

"The packets of photographs selected make it impossible to create seven 'traditional' families: that is, families that include a mother, a father, and children," says the curriculum guide.

"Students will find that they must create some families with adults of the same gender . . ." and then decide how to label the members.

The guide advises teachers to use their authority to encourage the right answer: "It is helpful for students if you use your own set of photos to create a family with two moms and/or two dads."

When the lesson is over, the teacher exhorts students to examine their beliefs, confess their errors, and commit to reform.

"Were there types of families that you didn't create?" asks the teacher. "Why do you think you didn't create those families?" (In other words, what's wrong with you?) "If you did this activity again, would you do anything differently?" (Hmm, I wonder what the right answer is to that one?)

"Welcoming Schools" uses the same strategy in its section on expanding "gender norms." (The guide advises teachers to avoid referring to their class as "boys and girls." "For some children," it explains, "identifying as a boy or girl in order to participate in an activity creates internal dissonance.") Students are evaluated on "whether or not they feel comfortable making choices outside gender expectations."

At Hale School, some parents are up in arms. While they oppose bullying, they say, this is not the way to address it. They have been explaining their concerns since February, when Principal Bob Brancale announced in an e-mail that "Welcoming Schools" "will be piloted . . . regardless of the personal issues or concerns of parents or staff."

"It's a direct slap at parents' faces," said Hale parent Arbuc Flomo of the newly formed Coalition for Parents' Rights." 'I used to think, but now I know . . .'? It's like a teacher saying to your first-grader, 'What you learned in your seven years before coming to first grade here—what you learned from your parents—is wrong.'"

Dan Loewenson of the Minneapolis School District says that parents are free to opt their children out of the program.

After Hale parents filed formal objections to "Welcoming Schools" in March, district leaders referred the matter to the district's Curriculum and Instruction Committee. On May 28, the committee will deliberate about the next steps after hearing from parents and staff.

The success of the homosexual propaganda program is based entirely on the claim that the point of these programs is to protect homosexual students from bullying. Kevin Jennings, the executive director of GLSEN, revealed in a 1995 speech how he used the issue of "safety" to delude then-governor William Weld and the state legislature into adopting the homosexual agenda for the schools of Massachusetts. "In Massachusetts the effective reframing of this issue was the key to the success of the Governor's Commission on Gay and Lesbian Youth. We immediately seized upon the opponent's calling card—safety. . . . Titling our report 'Making Schools Safe for Gay and Lesbian Youth,' we automatically threw our opponents onto the defensive and stole their best line of attack . . . and left them back-pedaling from day one."

Meanwhile, the homosecularists want to make schools unsafe for Christian students. If they succeed in redefining Christian teaching as bigotry, it is our children who will be bullied not only by other students but also by the schools and by the government itself.

Dr. Gary L. Cass is the president and CEO of the Christian Anti-Defamation Commission (CADC). He calls the political application of tolerance "a manipulative rhetoric that's used to try to make you seem unfair or narrow-minded if you happen to have strongly held beliefs." He points out that as a Christian, if you stand up, you are called every name in the book. "You're a bigot. You're a hatemonger." Isn't that an invitation to bullying and hatred and intolerance?

The largest teachers' union in the country, the National Education Association (NEA), is firmly allied with the homosecularists. In fact, former NEA president Bob Chase now serves on the board of GLSEN. The NEA's "diversity resolution" insists on teaching about sexual orientation and gender identification. These programs, as well as sex education, would be available without any parental notification. The NEA also lobbies for same-sex marriage.

How far do the homosecularists want to take homosexual in-doctrination of children?

Do I hear you saying, "OK, that's enough! I am pulling my kids out of public school and sending them to a Christian school tomorrow." That won't protect you when the IRS revokes your Christian school's tax-exempt status because it teaches Christian morality, which the government has redefined as bigotry. For that is exactly what safe schools curricula teach: your Christian beliefs are bigotry. It's only a matter of time before the government, pressured by the sex liberals, starts connecting the dots. Already, a California law forbids private schools from participating in inter-scholastic sporting events if they do not abide by certain "nondis-crimination" guidelines that really amount to endorsing sodomy.

American children are taught about homosexuality before they're even old enough to learn about sexuality. Meanwhile, you can't say the Lord's name in a public school. Christian faith is reg-ulated like obscenity while sexual perversion is encouraged, cele-brated, and glorified. The homosecularists know that if the next generation of Americans is raised to think that sodomy is the same as married love, then the battle will be over and our oppo-nents will have won.

CHAPTER FOUR

The ACLU v.
The U.S. Constitution

Liberal activist groups have used the courts for years to promote the destruction of traditional values and to silence people of faith. But now in increasing numbers, Christians are turning to the court system to protect themselves.

–JANET PARSHALL, FROM THE TV SERIES *SPEECHLESS*

One of the greatest successes that the secular liberals have achieved is convincing many, perhaps even most Americans that the Constitution forbids speaking about God in public facilities, especially public schools. The truth is nearly the opposite. Religious speech is especially protected under the First Amendment, not especially burdened as the secularists claim. And the courts, particularly the Supreme Court, whatever their other failings, have often done a good job of protecting religious speech. When Christians can force the ACLU and its allies into court to protect their rights, Christians win more often than they lose.

That's why the ACLU actually tries to avoid going to court. Its favorite tactic is to intimidate the schools and other public institutions into censoring Christian speech for fear of having to go to court itself. To make this tactic successful it has worked very hard to establish a myth known as "the wall of separation of church and state," which says Americans lose their right to speak up for their faith once they step on to public property. This myth has become so powerful that the secularists have actually convinced Americans to censor themselves or to submit meekly to public officials and legal activists who use it to shut down Christian speech.

The ACLU and its secularist allies do not practice constitutional interpretation; they practice constitutional intimidation. To see this up close, consider an amazing series of events in a couple of school districts in Texas.

Katy, Texas, is an affluent suburb of Houston with an extraordinary record of censoring Christians. Schools in Katy have banned Christmas songs; students were told that if they sang Christmas songs their grades would be affected negatively. Other Katy schools have tried to remove all references to Christmas in their district, and the colors red and green have been prohibited. Children have had their Bibles confiscated; the holy book was called "garbage" by administrators and thrown in the trash. In one instance, students were told they could not have book covers displaying the Ten Commandments because these laws of God were deemed to be hate speech[†].

Haley Pounds was a kindergartner in Pattison Elementary School in the Katy Independent School District in 2001. After the September 11, 2001, terrorist attacks, Haley's teacher had a discussion group in class and asked the students, "Why do you think 9/11 happened?" Several children shared their viewpoints or opinions. Then Haley spoke up and said, "Because God let it happen." Did the teacher empathize with Haley at that emotional moment? Apparently not. The teacher told Haley, "You know you can't talk about that at school. That's something you can talk about with your mom and dad."

When Haley arrived home from school that day, she shared the story with her mother, Dawn. Initially, Dawn didn't know how to handle the situation because Haley was her first child at Pattison Elementary, and she didn't want to seem like a troublemaker.

That same year, Dawn was homeroom mother. The year before, the school had held a Christmas party; this year, however, Patttison changed its policy and the party was now called a Winter party. When Dawn attended the homeroom-mother meeting, she was told that the party would be secular. Decorations like snowmen were allowed, but any religious symbols or references to religion would be prohibited. Even "Merry Christmas" would not be allowed.

When Dawn talked to the school principal, she said that the principal told her America was not founded on Christian principles and that the school needed to remain strictly neutral on any issues that might approach religion. Dawn pointed out, however, that other religions were allowed since children were doing projects on Kwanzaa, Ramadan, and Hanukkah.

In Pattison Elementary, censorship wasn't exclusive to Christmas. Natasha Gualy was a student in first grade and a member of a church group where she had made faith bracelets. Her Sunday school teacher said it would be fine if Natasha shared the bracelets with her friends at school. Natasha brought the bracelets with her to school and began passing them out to her friends at recess. The assistant principal saw what Natasha was doing and made her ask for all of her bracelets back and instructed her to tell her friends that it had been a mistake to give them out. Next, Natasha was told that she could never mention God's name at school again.

Students at Pattison have experienced a variety of different forms of bias. Here are just a few of the many incidents in both the parents' and students' own words:

• "We had free time and one of my Jewish friends was asking why I believed in Jesus. I was just telling her why when my teacher came up and told me we needed to talk about something else."

- "I got some [Gospel] tracts from church and the next day I brought them to school and asked my teacher if I could pass them out. She said, 'I don't know, let me think about it.' Later that day the principal came and took me out into the hall and said, 'You can't bring these to school because you're not allowed to talk about Jesus and God and Christian stuff.'"
- "Our pastor's daughter had brought some poems to school and they had to do with Jesus. Her father didn't even know she had them. She passed them out to her friends. And when the teacher figured out what they said, she made her go and pick them up and tell her daddy to keep his job at work. This is to a five-year old."
- "My teacher had some Christmas books and we all wanted to hear the one about Baby Jesus. She said, 'I don't want to read that one because I don't want to lose my job.'"

As president and chief counsel of Liberty Legal Institute, Kelly Shackelford points out these experiences can be very traumatic for children who feel as if they have been scolded for their beliefs and that they have done something wrong simply by mentioning Jesus. "A lot of times these kids go home crying." Shackelford says, "They are very young, impressionable kids. And when they get verbally whacked for mentioning God, it has a big impact on them."

In December 2002, Pattison Elementary held a fundraiser so that parents could purchase holiday cards decorated with their children's artwork. A form was sent home to parents with a selection of greetings they could have printed in the cards. There were two Hanukkah greetings, one Spanish greeting, a couple of Kwanzaa greetings, a generic "Happy Holidays," and the last option was Matthew 1:21, "And she shall bring forth a Son, and His name shall be called Jesus." But this was not a selection parents could choose. The scriptural passage was blacked out.

In another incident, some students were upset that they were not allowed to sing any songs with Christian themes during the Holiday concert of the school chorus. They then refused to sing songs that celebrated Hanukkah or Kwanzaa. However, the students who objected were told by the school administration that they were *required* to sing the songs of the other religions.

After years of discrimination against their Christian faith, parents in the Katy Independent School District filed a lawsuit in Harris County District Court to protect their children's rights. The parents and their lawyers from the Liberty Legal Institute expected the judge to rule using *Tinker v. Des Moines*, which is usually the controlling case dealing with student speech. But the judge didn't even mention *Tinker*. Instead, she used a case that dealt with the zoning restrictions of strip clubs.

That's right, the judge compared children sharing their religious beliefs at school with nude dancing! She concluded that if the state can restrict nude dancing, then it has the right to restrict students' free speech.

Katy isn't the only school district in Texas experiencing these problems. In the Plano Independent School District, just as in Katy, you can't have a Christmas party; it must be a Holiday party. No "Merry Christmas," and the colors red and green are excluded.

In Plano, children were told that they could not write "Merry Christmas" on cards that they were sending to American troops overseas. Other children who tried to hand out pencils that said "Jesus Loves You" to friends had them confiscated. A twelve-year-old girl who was waiting for her school bus outside the school after class hours began handing out her pencils to friends. The principal approached the student and confiscated every one of her pencils.

According to one affidavit, the superintendent of the Plano Independent School District said in a meeting with religious leaders that the district was "doing everything they could to shut down religious speech." And when he said *everything*, apparently he meant *everything including candy canes*.

During the Christmas, excuse me, "Holiday" season, a fourth-grade student brought some candy-cane writing pens to hand out to his classmates. The school stopped him from distributing them. Why? Because the candy cane's origin is Christian and was originally used as a Christian symbol.

Candy canes too religious? How did things get so bad?

In a coordinated effort to deny Christianity and other religions a place in American public life, liberal advocacy groups like the ACLU have argued that the First Amendment provides for a "wall of separation" between church and state. But this wall of separation is never mentioned in the Constitution. The phrase first appeared in a letter from Thomas Jefferson (who was out of the country serving as ambassador to France when the First Amendment was written) to the Danbury Baptist Association of Connecticut in 1802. The Danbury Baptists wanted reassurance from President Jefferson that there would be no state-established church and none of the persecution like that which they had suffered in England.

Jefferson replied that the government had no right to interfere in the religious opinions of its citizens. Referring to the First Amendment, he wrote: "I contemplate with sovereign reverence that act of the whole American people which declared that their legislature should make no law respecting the establishment of religion, or prohibiting the free exercise thereof, thus building a wall of separation between church and state." Then he went on to describe the amendment as the "expression of the supreme will of the nation in behalf of the rights of conscience . . ."†

This is clearly the letter of a man who wishes to protect religious freedom not restrict it. How are the "rights of conscience" advanced by punishing children for singing Christmas songs or telling them that their beliefs have no place in a discussion of 9/11?

The secularists have been so successful in spreading their myth of a wall of separation of church and state that many Americans are convinced that public expressions of religion are un-American. Ignorance of the law is no excuse, however, for the actions of the ACLU and other secular legal groups. They know very well that according to Supreme Court precedent a government action that imposes a significant burden on religious practice can only be justified if it advances "a compelling state interest" and "no alternative forms of regulation" are available. Both standards need to be met. This legal concept is known as "strict scrutiny" and was written by none other than liberal Supreme Court Justice William Brennan. The goal is to establish a powerful presumption on behalf of religious belief and expression and against government censorship or regulation. As Supreme Court Justice Antonin Scalia has written, "Our precedent establishes that private religious speech, far from being a First Amendment orphan, is as fully protected under the Free Speech Clause as secular private expression. . . . Indeed, in Anglo-American history, at least, government suppression of speech has so commonly been directed precisely at religious speech that a free-speech clause without religion would be Hamlet without the prince."

The law is clear. But many school administrators aren't following the law because they don't know it. And they fear that tolerating religious speech will cost the schools precious dollars meant for education. As John W. Whitehead of the Rutherford

Institute points out, "Taxpayers have to pay for the legal battles that never should have been fought in the first place," even if they win. And when the ACLU wins a case they often "sue for the taxpayers to reimburse their legal fees. Funds that should have been used for student activities are spent on legal fees." The root problem, as Whitehead says, is that many "public school officials are just ignorant" about the First Amendment. "When they say something's illegal, they're just repeating something that they've heard from a secular group."

> Many of the experts we've spoken with say parents are intimidated by school officials. They view them as authority figures because it's assumed these people know the law. But these same experts report that in a great many instances, the official may in fact be ignorant of the law and just stating a policy. No policy can ever trump the rights guaranteed by the Constitution.
>
> Janet Parshall, from the TV series *Speechless*

This is what happens. The ACLU either gets a complaint or finds out about an alleged violation of its imaginary wall of separation in a public school. Then ACLU lawyers write a threatening letter to the school administration, claiming, in typical lawyerly bombast, that the law has been broken and great harm has been done. They warn that if the administration doesn't rectify the situation there will be no end of trouble. The school administrators either don't know the law or don't want the hassle. So they cave in to the ACLU.

Or at least the ACLU hopes they will cave in. For when Christians fight back, they often win. Sometimes you don't even need to go to court. By just showing up at school board meetings, Christian parents can exert pressure on administrators and push back against ACLU threats. In Texas, Christians fought back big time and won hands down.

Don't Mess with Texas

Because Christians fought back, on June 11, 2007, Governor Rick Perry signed into law a bill that will protect the rights of students in Texas public schools to express their religious beliefs.

Here is how the law reads:

A school district shall treat a student's voluntary expression of a religious viewpoint, if any, on an otherwise permissible subject, in the same manner the district treats a student's voluntary expression of a secular or other viewpoint on an otherwise permissible subject, and may not discriminate against the student based on a religious viewpoint expressed by the student on an otherwise permissible subject.

Religious Viewpoints Antidiscrimination Act,
aka the Schoolchildren's Religious Liberties Act

The Texas law (whose precedent is the 1990 Supreme Court case *Board of Westside Community Schools v. Mergens*) makes it very clear that when students speak in a public setting any religious content of their speech is protected by the free-expression clause. If school administrators are afraid that such expressions might be construed as official endorsement of those individual views, they can provide a disclaimer that makes clear that the student is speaking as an individual and not as a representative of the school.

One of the driving forces behind this law was Kelly Coghlan, a Houston attorney who specializes in religious liberty issues. Coghlan was just another trial lawyer when he received a phone call from a junior high school student who was vice president of the student council. As part of her council duties, the student gave morning announcements, which she liked to open with a positive and inspirational quote. One day, when she read from the Old Testament, the school principal told her that the one source she couldn't use for her quotes was the Bible.

"Is that legal?" the girl asked Coghlan. Coghlan began studying the issue. Soon he discovered how widespread the problem was. Coghlan was surprised how ignorance and intimidation had allowed Christians to be silenced. And he didn't understand why people could be so sensitive as to be grievously offended by any mention of religion or Christian heritage. How does saying "Merry Christmas" hurt anybody? As Coghlan says, "Kids believe in Santa Claus. Now, if I don't believe in Santa Claus do I get offended? I may chuckle. I may laugh. If I pray in the name of Jesus Christ, why don't you just chuckle or laugh to yourself and say, 'You know, that's like Santa Claus' but don't be offended. . . . We need to loosen up a little bit in America."

Coghlan's work on religious liberty led him to help draft the Texas law. By codifying case law, the Texas legislation gives school administrations, parents, and students the ability to understand the legal parameters without first having to consult a lawyer and to defend themselves from groups like the ACLU.

During hearings on the bill, a representative from the ACLU spoke first. The organization opposed the bill, but they weren't really sure why. "It was just sort of a gut reaction," Coghlan recalls. Once the rest of the evidence was presented, including testimony from constitutional attorneys and students who had been the victims of discrimination, a prominent local ACLU attorney told Coghlan that he didn't realize how many students were being denied the right to free speech, and he was going to talk to the national leadership and try to convince them to support this type of legislation. Apparently his efforts didn't go far, as the ACLU remains opposed to religious freedom legislation like the Texas law.

In 2007, Texas was the first state to adopt the Schoolchildren's Religious Liberties Act, as drafted by Coghlan, to give equal protection, freedom, and opportunity to students of faith attending public schools. Now that the law has been passed, students can discuss religious matters or their own beliefs in school. They can use religious texts in their assignments if applicable to the subject matter.

The law includes a suggested model policy that protects the districts and the taxpayers from undue legal action by guaranteeing that if the district adopts the model policy, the attorney general of Texas will defend the district against any legal challenges†.

The model policy clearly protects students from censorship on the basis of content discrimination. If students are selected to speak based on neutral criteria—like being class valedictorians or star athletes—they must stick to the permissible subject of their speech, such as academic success or sportsmanship, for example. Within those basic parameters, the student has the right to interject religious references, Bible quotations, or stories of personal inspiration or belief. If a student believes his faith in Jesus Christ helped his academic success or sportsmanship, he can say so. As long as students do not stray from the permissible subject, they may not be discriminated against by the government because of any religious content in their speeches.

A full-text version of the legislation can be found at www.christianattorney.com/texasact.htm. You can download it, print it out, and show it to your local representative.

We're hoping what we did here will be a springboard and a great help to everybody across the country.

Kelly Coghlan, author of the
Schoolchildren's Religious Liberties Act

In Texas there are 4.5 million public school children whose constitutional rights of religious freedom are now protected and reinforced by state law. There are approximately forty-five million other students in public schools all across America who have the same rights but may not know it.

CHAPTER FIVE

Some Religions Are More Equal than Others

Don't be surprised if one day you hear the muezzin calling for prayer and saying 'Allahu Akbar' from the top of the White House. September 11 is Allah's work against oppressors.

—Sheik Taj Al-Din Hamed Abdallah Al-Hilali, mufti of Australia and New Zealand

The push for tolerance of other faiths has resulted in a culture of intolerance for Christians.

—Janet Parshall, from the TV series *Speechless*

When liberals say they want to keep religion out of public schools, they really mean they want to exclude Christianity.

That's clear when other religions, particularly Islam, are encouraged, supported, and even practiced in public school curricula.

The Pacific Justice Institute, of Santa Ana, California, has performed an extensive investigation of religious bias in school textbooks. The organization found that several books "sanitize the problems of Islam" while being highly critical of Christian and Western culture. Although the texts focus on the history of American slavery and denying women the right to vote until the early twentieth century, subjects like jihad and Islamic violence, the imposition of sharia law, the record of Muslim enslavement, and the subjection of women are "glossed over."

One textbook in particular has generated a great deal of concern among those who fear that our schoolchildren aren't learning the whole truth about Islam. *Across the Centuries* is a history textbook used in nearly every seventh-grade class in California. The book contains outright propaganda for Islam, claiming, for example, that Islam is what has liberated women and given them equal rights. There is no mention of Islamic extremism, the brutality of sharia law, or the subjugation of women. And while Islam is consistently portrayed in a positive light, Christianity is seen negatively.

Here are just a few examples:

- Discussing why Jerusalem is so important to world religions, the textbook says, "Jerusalem is where Jesus was crucified and buried, and it was where Muhammad rose to heaven." While Muhammad is deified, the book makes no mention of Jesus' resurrection and ascension.
- The text fails to mention that Islam allows polygamy.
- In clear contradiction of the rules imposed on the description of Christianity in history texts, the book refers to expressions of belief as statements of historical fact when discussing Islam. "[T]he very first word the Angel Gabriel spoke to Muhammad was 'recite.'"
- Describing the life of Muhammad, the text tries to downplay his role as a leader in holy warfare against those of other faiths. Instead, it claims "Muhammad's success in spreading Islam was due in large part to his strong character, morality, courage, and compassion."
- The book does not mention that Muhammad owned slaves and was a slave trader.
- In a section discussing religious persecution, the only acts of persecution are those committed by Christians. The atrocities

of other religions throughout history (and even today) are conveniently ignored.

This is not just biased history but unconstitutional privileging of one religion over another. If ever there were a First Amendment Establishment Clause violation, *Across the Centuries* certainly qualifies. As the Pacific Justice Institute notes, "Although it is not unconstitutional for schools to teach about different religions, established case law requires that such instruction be neither hostile nor preferential toward any particular faith. In other words, religious instruction must be balanced."

While school textbooks celebrate Islam, the Christian roots of American history have been systematically erased from many textbooks used in public schools.

According to David Limbaugh in his book *Persecution: How Liberals Are Waging A War Against Christianity*, The New Jersey Department of Education removed all references to the Pilgrims and the *Mayflower* from their standards for history texts because of their religious connotations. At the first Thanksgiving, the Pilgrims are not described as giving thanks to God but merely as "giving thanks for all they had."

"It is common in these books," found a study by New York University psychology professor Paul C. Vitz, "to treat Thanksgiving without explaining to whom the Pilgrims gave thanks. The Pueblo [Indians] can pray to Mother Earth, but the Pilgrims can't be described as praying to God—and never are Christians described as praying to Jesus."

Amazingly, some schools are actually making children practice Islam. After 9/11 several California schools adopted a program described as a "simulation of the history and culture of Islam." But it was nothing less than indoctrination into the Muslim religion. This is what a student guide to the curriculum actually said: "From the beginning, you and your classmates will become Muslims."

Simulation or Indoctrination?

For fifteen days, students were required to follow Muslim habits and rituals. They dressed in Muslim clothing and took on Muslim names. They recited verses from the Koran and were made to say other Muslim prayers. They even participated in their own jihads.

Students were not given any choice: they couldn't opt out of the program and their performances affected their grades. If they didn't memorize their Koranic verses well enough, or didn't answer to their adopted Muslim names, they could get graded negatively.

In spite of daily violence around the world committed by radical Islamists, the California students were taught that jihad means doing "one's best to resist temptation and overcome evil," thereby downplaying any pervasive violence. Students were even encouraged to stage their own jihads as an exercise for the class.†

A blatant and consistent ideological bias informed the curriculum. Students were not only taught about Islam but also made to practice the religion itself. They recited Muslim prayers that began with "In the name of Allah, Most Gracious, Most Merciful." They memorized the Muslim profession of faith: "Allah is the only true God and Muhammad his messenger." They were asked to read and analyze Koranic scriptures and chanted, "Praise be to Allah" in response to promptings from their teachers. And they professed as "true" the belief that "the Holy Koran is God's word."

Not surprisingly, some Christian students and their parents objected to the "Islamic simulation." The Thomas More Law

Center, a national public interest law firm located in Ann Arbor, Michigan, represented Jonas and Tiffany Eklund on behalf of their two children, Chase and Samantha, who were students at Excelsior Middle School in the Byron Union School District in Byron, California. When a lower court, presided over by a Clinton-appointed judge, found that the simulation did not violate the Establishment Clause because the students were "role playing" and "simulating" professions of faith, the United States Court of Appeals for the Ninth District upheld that ruling. This is the same court that outlawed the Pledge of Allegiance in public schools.

This program was just a *simulation*. A growing number of American public schools with significant Muslim populations are facilitating and encouraging Islam in ways they would never support Christianity.

Carver Elementary School in San Diego, California, includes students from kindergarten to eighth grade. The school population was originally three hundred, but when a magnet school serving a Somali Muslim population failed, Carver accepted one hundred of these students. At first, the Muslim students were treated like a special elite, given a fifteen-minute recess to pray during the school day, and even being led in prayer by a teacher's aide. Gradually, the other students were affected by this special treatment. Now, Christmas at the school is called "Winter Holiday Celebration" so that non-Christian students will not be offended. Muslim and African traditions are celebrated while Christian traditions are avoided.

At Carver Elementary, classes were segregated along gender lines in keeping with Islamic tradition. Foods that were not approved in the Islamic religion were removed from the cafeteria menu, and a special room was set aside for a daily hour of Islamic prayer, chants, and meditations.† If Christian students were allowed to worship on taxpayer-funded property during school hours, liberal groups would be outraged.

Islam in public schools is not just happening in California. In September 2007, New York City established an Islamic public school: the Khalil Gibran International Academy teaches its students in Arabic. While its administrators and supporters claim that there will be no religious or political indoctrination, many critics argue that an ideological message of pro-Muslim, anti-American propaganda will most assuredly be taught, especially since the school's top administrators have ties to organizations that have supported radical Islamists.

Extremism on Campus

The atmosphere found on college and univeristy campuses is among the most consistently anti-Christian and pro-Muslim in American public life. Particularly after the terrorist attacks of September 11, professors and administrators at our institutions of higher education have consistently promoted Islam while censoring anything that smacked of Christianity.

Every year, the University of North Carolina at Chapel Hill gives a summer reading assignment to its incoming freshmen and transfer students who are asked to read an assigned book and write a short paper over the summer, then attend seminars to discuss the book when they arrive in the fall at the university.

Over the summer of 2002, the required reading was *Approaching the Qur'an*, a book of selected excerpts and exegesis of the Islamic holy book, along with a CD of calls to prayer and readings in Arabic. Explaining this policy, the university's Web site described the "enduring interest" of the work and called Islam a "profound moral and spiritual tradition."

Imagine what would have happened if a state university like

UNC-Chapel Hill had required its students to read the Bible, appealing to its "enduring interest" and calling Christianity a "profound moral and spiritual tradition." The ACLU would have that school in federal court before you could say, "Allahu Akbar" or, "Praise the Lord and pass the ammunition," whichever you prefer.

While the ACLU remained silent on the issue, a group of Christian students and alumni took a page from the ACLU's playbook. They filed a lawsuit, arguing that the required reading of a religious text by a state school violated the Establishment Clause of the First Amendment. Eventually, the North Carolina state legislature voted to cut off university funding for the program. The university found outside funding, and the Christian students' lawsuit was rejected by the United States Court of Appeals for the Fourth Circuit. (On March 3, 2006, Mohammad Taheri-azar, a 2005 UNC-Chapel Hill Iranian graduate student rented an SUV from a local rental company and rammed the vehicle into nine pedestrians at The Pit, a popular and crowded campus location, to "avenge the death of Muslims around the world.")

Apparently it's OK to promote Islam in public schools and colleges, but don't get caught criticizing it. The Foundation for Individual Rights in Education (FIRE), a nonpartisan, ecumenical organization that fights for liberty of expression in colleges and universities, has reported the following cases:

- Orange Coast Community College in Costa Mesa, California, suspended Professor Kenneth W. Hearlson without a hearing when Muslim students complained about his lecture in a contemporary politics course when he argued that silence on crimes against Christians and Jews in the Middle East was consent to terrorism.

- A political science major at San Diego State University was formally admonished for arguing with four Saudi Arabian students who were "delighted" about the September 11 attacks.
- Duke University shut down Professor Gary Hull's Web site after he posted an article calling for a strong military response to the terrorist attacks. The university later reinstated the Web site on the condition that Hull add a disclaimer making clear that his views did not reflect those of Duke, something that is not required of any other professor.

Ultimately we [Muslims] can never be full citizens of this country ... because there is no way we can be fully committed to the institutions and ideologies of this country.

Ihsan Bagby, associate professor of
Islamic Studies at University of Kentucky

The sympathy that the ACLU and its homosexual allies have for radical Islam is not only troubling but also curious. You might think that a political movement focused on forcing religion out of the public sphere would stand in direct opposition to Islam, which even in its more moderate strains insists on the primacy of religious faith. Not to mention the fact that under Muslim sharia law homosexual behavior is a capital crime. But the radical Left has an instinctive tendency to join sides with those who are opposed to Christianity. If someone hates America, the Left is on his side.

Discrimination in schools against Christian students may have started out innocently as an effort to prevent discrimination of students of other faiths, but this policy of inclusion has snowballed into a doctrine of silence for the Christian students.

Janet Parshall, from the TV series *Speechless*

A nation that cannot distinguish between its own vital traditions and that of the enemies who wish to destroy it lacks the most basic means of self-defense. If our children and grandchildren are taught that Islam is superior to Christianity and that they are supposed to remain silent, to not complain when strange faiths are forced upon them or when their religion is disparaged, how can we possibly expect to win the war on terror? And how can we possibly ask them to fight it?

Privileging other religions over Christianity has become second nature in our educational institutions. It's not just Islam. Sometimes Christianity is silenced in favor of witchcraft, as we will see in the next story.

All About Me

In Wesley Busch's kindergarten class, in Newtown Square, Pennsylvania, it was his turn to celebrate "All About Me" week.† During their special week, students were invited to bring in their favorite food, toy, or stuffed animal. Parents were also encouraged to participate: they could make a poster describing different things their child liked or read from their child's favorite book.

Wesley Busch had asked his mother Donna to read from the Bible, which she was very happy to do. When her turn came, she told the teacher she was going to read a few verses from Psalm 118.

Give thanks unto the Lord, for He is good;
   because His mercy endures for ever.
Let Israel now say,
   that His mercy endures for ever.
Let the house of Aaron now say
   that His mercy endures for ever.

Let them now that fear the Lord say
    that His mercy endures for ever....
The Lord is my strength and song
    and is become my salvation.

Psalm 118:1-4, 14

Donna had chosen these Bible verses because she and Wesley frequently read from the Bible together at breakfast and before bedtime, and Wesley particularly liked the Psalms. She thought that the other children in Wesley's class would enjoy them because they were like poetry or songs. She specifically chose an Old Testament reading because she knew the school had a history of hostility towards Christianity, and she didn't want to select a reading that mentioned Christ.

As soon as the teacher heard that Donna wanted to read from the Bible, she interrupted, saying that she would have to speak to the principal. The teacher returned to the classroom and asked Donna to step out into the hallway. The principal was very upset that Donna had brought a Bible into the school. He explained that reading the Bible in class would be "against the law . . . of separation of church and state." The children in that room would be a captive audience. It would be as if Donna were trying to convert them to Christianity, "promoting a specific religious point of view."

The principal and the teacher offered Donna an alternative to reading from the Bible. They told her that since it was Halloween season, she could read about witches, black cats, and demons. But she could not read from the Bible. The principal, talking very loudly, appeared agitated and upset. The classroom door had been left open during the adults' discussion, and the students in the classroom had heard what had been said.

Feeling that something should be done, Donna contacted the Rutherford Institute. With the Alliance Defense Fund, the

Rutherford Institute filed a lawsuit arguing that the school administrators violated Donna's "First Amendment right to free speech, discriminated against her speech on the basis of its religious viewpoint, and deprived her of the right to equal protection under the law as guaranteed by the Fourteenth Amendment to the United States Constitution."

The judge took a year to decide. Then, in a thirty-nine-page opinion, he ruled that the school had not been guilty of violating Wesley and Donna Busch's rights. The judge decided that in order to avoid endorsing any kind of religious activity, the school had the right to censor free speech and religious expression based on "a compelling interest."

So Donna could have read about witches and demons, though both witchcraft and devil worship are religions. And judging by the trend in public schools, it would have been OK for Donna to read from the Koran. And yet we are told that the state has a "compelling interest" in forbidding a mother to read the Psalms.

What do you suppose that compelling interest might be?

CHAPTER SIX

Leviathan v. The Boy Scouts

The state is jealous of any God and continually seeks to limit belief and allegiance to anybody or anything but itself.

—JIM DEMINT AND J. DAVID WOODARD,
*WHY WE WHISPER, RESTORING OUR
RIGHT TO SAY IT'S WRONG*

J oseph Kinney is a Vietnam War veteran suffering from the effects of Agent Orange exposure. He receives treatment at his local VA medical center in Fayetteville, North Carolina. He regularly visits the hospital's chapel to read the Bible and pray. But one day, when he went to the chapel, he saw that both the Bible and the altar's cross were missing.[†]

He looked around the chapel and found the Bible and the cross on the floor, so he picked them up and placed them back on the altar. A few minutes later, a gentleman entered the chapel and asked Kinney how those items wound up on the altar.

"I put them there," Kinney replied.

"Well, I'm ordering you to take them down because you didn't have the authority put them up," the man said.

"I don't care. I'm not taking them down. That's where they belong. They belong on the altar."

"Then I'm going to have you arrested."

"That's fine with me," Kinney said. "You can have me arrested if you want."

The man angrily took the Bible and the cross from the altar and threw them on the ground. Then he told Kinney to come with him. Kinney followed the man into his office where he told Kinney about "the neutralization policy" and how the symbols of Christianity were going to be removed from the chapel.

The U.S. Department of Veterans Affairs had issued a neutralization policy for the chapel, which included such requirements as removal of the cross, the Bible, and pictures of Jesus Christ from the altar, as well as a signed pledge by volunteer chaplains that they would not mention the name of Jesus while they ministered to patients. Stained-glass windows in the chapel were covered with paper shades.†

A Catholic display, including a cross, a kneeler, and a Bible, were allowed to remain in the chapel on the condition that they were partitioned off from the main part of the room. All of the items that were taken away, partitioned off, or hidden had been donated by individuals or organizations such as the Knights of Columbus. None of them had been provided by government funds. Programs involving local church volunteers who came to serve communion were terminated. The chaplain was placed on administrative leave.

> I'm a Christian today because a priest came to me on the battlefield. What's happened at Fayetteville could become a disease, a cancer. It could strike at Christianity not only throughout the VA system but also in the military. So if we don't speak up and get involved, then we're aiding and abetting the destruction of Christianity in the Veterans Administration [Veterans Affairs Department] and potentially the Department of Defense.
>
> Joseph Kinney, Vietnam War veteran

According to the new regulations, patients and visitors can *request* a Bible or a cross while they are worshipping in the chapel.

But what happens to the wounded soldier who can't sleep and wants to pray in the chapel? Kinney himself has been in the VA chapel in Fayetteville when he couldn't find anyone to provide him with a Bible or a cross. And this was in the middle of a weekday. Technically, the VA can claim it is not forbidding Christians to worship according to their consciences, but the government certainly has gone to a lot of effort to make it harder.

> [T]he VA has trampled on the needs of Christian and Catholic veterans in order to meet the 'requirements' of some unidentified third party that would be offended by a Bible or a cross. . . . I fought for freedom, not the suppression of freedom. No Muslim, Hindu, or Buddhist has called me to tell me that I am jeopardizing his religious practice by insisting that there be a Christian chapel at the VA. In fact, some worry that there will be a backlash against their interests.
>
> Joseph Kinney

Why would the VA push to "neutralize" the chapels in its hospitals? Who exactly is complaining about the presence of Bibles or crosses in VA chapels? Actually, no one. The VA was not asked by any veterans, or anyone else for that matter, to remove the Bible and cross from its chapels. The VA apparently changed the policy in anticipation that someone or some organization *might* object. The VA was nervous about something that *might* happen—not something that had happened—so nervous, in fact, that VA administrators even told Kinney that he was not "authorized" to discuss the chapel neutralization policy with anyone while he was on hospital grounds.

Call it "censorship by anticipation." Public institutions censor Christian speech, even when no citizen has objected and even when, as so many court cases ultimately reflect, the law is actually on the side of the Christians. It is a huge problem.

This didn't happen by accident. It is exactly what the ACLU and its allies aim to do with their policy of threatening schools and other public organizations with legal action and other harassment, even though the anti-Christian forces often know they would or could lose in court. The parents don't know that; the school board may not know it. And thanks to the constant barrage from the ACLU and its pals, lots of Americans have gotten a vague impression that they have a lot less religious liberty than they actually do. So they think "better safe than sorry" and begin censoring themselves. The ACLU thinks that is a beautiful thing.

The ACLU has repeatedly tried to eliminate religious expression in the United States military. The group has already stopped mealtime prayers at the Virginia Military Institute and has been fighting for years to keep midshipmen at the U.S. Naval Academy from saying grace at lunchtime, a tradition that dates back to the founding of that institute.

Complaints about religious content even led to a ban on flag-folding recitations by Veterans Affairs employees and volunteers at all national cemeteries. At thousands of military burials, VA volunteers folded the American flag thirteen times and recited the significance of each fold to survivors. The eleventh fold glorifies "the God of Abraham, Isaac, and Jacob." The twelfth glorifies "God the Father, the Son, and the Holy Ghost."

Following one complaint, the Veterans Affairs banned that recitation. Citing a need for uniformity, the National Cemetery Administration prohibited unpaid VA volunteers as well as employees from conducting the recital at all one hundred twenty-five national cemeteries.

We at the American Family Association (AFA) fought back. In response to our campaign, the Department of Veterans Affairs reversed its ruling, and now the traditional flag-folding ceremony is available for Christian burials.

But what if we hadn't been there? I don't mean that in a bragging way. But it is important for Christians to realize two things. First, the battle for religious speech is not just a lawyers' technical battle; it is a battle within the culture, a battle of education. Second, it doesn't matter how many court cases we win if the anti-Christians persuade law-abiding Americans or public officials to believe that censorship is the law.

Often "censorship by anticipation" is not caused because of the fear of a lawsuit but simply because of the fear of "offending someone." Recently our nation's legislators were prohibited from making references to God (such as "God bless you" or "In the year of our Lord") in certificates of authenticity accompanying flags flown over the Capitol and purchased by constituents. Stephen T. Ayers, of the Architect of the Capitol (the agency responsible for the maintenance, operation, and preservation of the U.S. Capitol Complex), said he had removed the words because reference to God and the Lord may offend some Americans.

The National Park Service (NPS) censored God from a key display of America's Christian heritage in Washington. On the aluminium cap that sits atop the Washington Monument are engraved the words *Laus Deo* (Praise [be] to God). Of course, visitors can't see the actual cap because it is 555 feet above the ground. The display materials below have always shown pictures of the cap with the inscription—until recently when the NPS censored it. Now children and other visitors to the monument have no way of knowing that atop our nation's greatest monument is inscribed a prayer of praise. No wonder Americans have slowly but surely been given the impression that "the American way" is to push religion underground.

An e-mail campaign by AFA supporters forced the government to rescind that order.

But of course there was no good reason in the first place for censoring the materials, not even a legal pretense. No court forced the National Park Service to do so. What has happened is that anti-Christians, even though they often lose in court, are using the courts and fear of the courts to put us Christians on the defensive. The law, including false impressions about what the law says, shapes the culture.

A recent, very sad example of this has been the relentless assault on the Boy Scouts, one of the great institutions in American life, and a group that we need now more than ever.

The Boy Scouts of America was founded in 1910 and quickly earned the encouragement and support of all levels of American government. In 1916, the Scouts received a charter from the U.S. Congress. The president of the United States traditionally serves as the Scouts' honorary chairman. More than one hundred ten million Americans have served as Boy Scouts, including an amazing number of civic leaders and public servants. A majority of graduates of the military service academies were Boy Scouts, as were 85 percent of FBI agents and two-thirds of all astronauts, including eleven of the twelve men who walked on the moon.

The Boy Scouts stands for much of what is good about America—hard work, cheerfulness, thrift, community service, helping others. The Scouts makes no apologies about the fact that its organization was founded on strong Christian values and remains faithful to them.

> On my honor I will do my best
> To do my duty to God and my country
> And to obey the Scout Law;
> To help other people at all times;

To keep myself physically strong,
mentally awake, and morally straight.

The Scout Oath (or Promise)

A Scout is trustworthy, loyal, helpful, friendly, courteous,
kind, obedient, cheerful, thrifty, brave, clean, and reverent.

The Scout Law

The ACLU doesn't like the idea that the Scouts practice
Christian values. The organization has repeatedly sued the Scouts
because the group refuses to admit openly homosexual Scouts or
adult leaders. Now if that rule seems harsh to you, remember that
"openly homosexual," practically speaking, means sexually active.
Ask yourself, "Would I really be happy sending my eleven-year-
old son, just going through puberty, full of normal, adolescent
sexual anxiety and confusion, on an all-male camping trip led by
scoutmasters who are sexually active sodomites or even accompa-
nied by sodomite senior Scouts (who can be as old as eighteen)?"

Practically speaking, how long would scouting last if the Boy
Scouts became known as a playground for homosexuals seeking
teen boys for sex? And before you tell me, "But gay men aren't
the same as pedophiles," pedophilia has nothing to do with it.
Scouts are pubescent or post-pubescent males and thus attractive
to many "normal" homosexuals.

This fear is not just hypothetical. Though not as widely reported as similar scandals in the Catholic Church, the Boy Scouts
organization was struggling against a dramatic increase in sexual
abuse cases, peaking at about two hundred per year in the late
1990s.

In a culture that increasingly sexualizes children and seeks
to normalize homosexuality, no wonder the Scouts hold

tight to their exclusionary policy. Parents won't entrust their kids to the Scouts' care if the organization can't guarantee their safety. For the homosexual activists, what percentage of sexually abused kids would be an acceptable trade-off against the self-esteem of homosexual scoutmasters? To any reasonable American, and certainly to any parent, the answer is zero.

Stefan Kanfer, *City Journal*

Unfortunately, the Boy Scouts has become a classic case of Christians winning the main issue in the courts but being devastated, punished, censored, and marginalized anyway.

One legal case of a Scout leader who lost his position when he publicly announced his homosexuality made it all the way to the Supreme Court. In *Boy Scouts of America v. Dale*, the court decided in favor of the Scouts, ruling that the organization's ability to limit its membership was guaranteed by the constitutional right to free association. Finding that the Boy Scouts' goal was to "instill values in young people," the court determined that such a mission was a form of expression, and therefore their membership rules were "expressive association."

We are not, as we must not be, guided by our views of whether the Boy Scouts' teachings with respect to homosexual conduct are right or wrong; public or judicial disapproval of a tenet of an organization's expression does not justify the state's effort to compel the organization to accept members where such acceptance would derogate from the organization's expressive message. 'While the law is free to promote all sorts of conduct in place of harmful behavior, it is not free to interfere with speech for no better reason than promoting an approved message or discouraging a disfavored one, however enlightened either purpose may strike the government.'

Boy Scouts of America v. Dale, Chief Justice William
Rehnquist writing for the majority (2000)

The *Dale* decision should have been a major victory for the Scouts. Yet instead of accepting the ruling and allowing the Scouts to continue its traditional policies, the homosecularists went on a counterattack waging legal, political, economic, and propaganda warfare.

One tactic the homosecularists love to use is, "OK, maybe the First Amendment allows the Boy Scouts to choose its own leaders, just like a church can choose its own pastors. But the church doesn't get to use public facilities for religion, and now that the Boy Scouts are considered 'bigots,' they don't get to use public facilities either, nor can they be sponsored or assisted by government in any way." The American Civil Liberties Union, for instance, has sued various government agencies to keep them from supporting or even being involved with scouting. As a result of one ACLU legal assault, the Department of Defense no longer sponsors Scout units, and the ACLU tried unsuccessfully to terminate the long-standing tradition of holding Boy Scout jamborees on military bases.

Cities all across the nation began placing restrictions on local Scout organizations. Chicago, San Francisco, and San Jose no longer allow local Boy Scout chapters to use public facilities without charge, including city parks. San Francisco judges are not allowed to be involved with the Boy Scouts. Following a three-year legal battle, San Diego canceled its park lease with the Scouts and wound up reimbursing the ACLU more than three-quarters of a million dollars in legal fees for lawsuits against the Scouts. Many school boards prevent the Boy Scouts from using school facilities or recruiting in schools.

All of this happened after the Scouts won its case in the Supreme Court.

See what happens? Sure, the BSA is "free" to act according to its principles. But because the homosecularists define Scout principles as bigotry, Boy Scouts are excluded from "the public square," any place or institution owned or controlled by government at any level or that even does much of its business with government. That's a lot of space, especially for the Boy Scouts, potentially including every national and state park. What would Teddy Roosevelt, founder of the National Park System, think about excluding the nation's largest organization dedicated to male leadership and the "vigorous life" that he advocated, from national parks because it did not want to expose its young members to lonely sodomites?

> Since we were founded, we believe that open homosexuality would be inconsistent with the values that we want to communicate with our leaders. A belief in God is also mentioned in the Scouts oath. We believe that those values are important. Tradition is important. Our mission is to instill those values in Scouts and help them make good choices over their lifetimes.
>
> Gregg Shields, spokesman for Boy Scouts of America

As usual, it has not stopped with just the government. The government forms and legitimizes the public culture. Soon organizations affiliated with the United Way were urged to stop supporting the Boy Scouts. Filmmaker Steven Spielberg, a former Scout himself, quit the advisory board because he said he could no longer be associated with an organization that discriminated. Numerous corporations were pressured into dropping their support for the Scouts, including Wells Fargo, Chase Manhattan

Bank, Levi Strauss, Carrier, and Textron. The labor union Communications Workers of America severed all ties with the BSA.

One of the saddest stories in the Scout saga involves the Philadelphia chapter, among the nation's oldest. The city of Philadelphia informed the Cradle of Liberty Boy Scouts Council that unless the organization changed its national policy and began admitting openly homosexual Scout leaders, the Scouts would have to leave its headquarters in the historic Beaux-Arts building on Museum Row.

Now this is not any ordinary public building. It is a building the Boy Scouts had constructed with its own funds, as well as paid for all its maintenance. In effect, the building was a gift to the city from the Scouts. The property belongs to the city, based on a 1928 agreement that the city would lease it to the Scouts for a symbolic one dollar a year in perpetuity, as long as the property was used for scouting activities. The Philadelphia chapter was the seventh largest in the BSA and had a long tradition of community service.

On May 31, 2007, the Philadelphia City Council voted 16–1 to terminate the Scouts' lease unless the organization began admitting homosexuals. The rationale behind this vote was that the city council would not "subsidize" a group that went against city policy in discriminating against homosexuals. In October, the city announced a new fee for the Scouts' lease: $200,000 annually, the equivalent of eight hundred disadvantaged children going to Scout-sponsored summer camp. Having already lost support from crucial donors such as United Way because of pressure from homosexual activists, there was no way the Scouts could afford to pay. Now the city would be free to sell the building to the highest bidder.

There are some sixty-four thousand Boy Scouts in Philadelphia, providing services to an additional estimated forty thousand local youths in programs that range from after-school mentoring to job shadowing. According to a study by researchers at the University of Pennsylvania, if the social services provided free of charge by the Boy Scouts were taken over by other organizations, it would cost the city an estimated $250 million a year.

While the city of Philadelphia does everything it can to undermine the Boy Scouts, its youth are in danger. Nearly 30 percent of the children in Philadelphia live in poverty. There are almost four thousand homeless families in the city. Barely half the city's ninth graders graduate from high school within four years. In 2006, 179 children were murdered. Surely there is a role for the Boy Scouts in Philadelphia.

When the eviction was first announced, citizens sent so many angry messages that they crashed the e-mail system of the Philadelphia mayor's office. Some one hundred fifty thousand Scout-related messages were deleted from the city's e-mail system.

"We were deluged," said Terry Phillis, Philadelphia's chief information officer. "We pulled the messages off so they wouldn't take the system down. It had to be done to protect the system's integrity."

Or maybe the city didn't want any documentary evidence of the public outrage.

The Threat of Prison Fellowship

Chuck Colson was the chief counsel for President Richard Nixon. He served seven months in prison for planning a break-in at Daniel Ellsberg's psychiatrist's office. After his release from prison, Chuck Colson founded Prison Fellowship, a faith-based organization that partners with local churches to work with prisoners, ex-prisoners, and their families.

In 2003, Americans United for Separation of Church and State filed a lawsuit against Prison Fellowship, claiming that the organization's partial funding from tax dollars violated the Constitution. The lawsuit focused on the InnerChange Freedom Initiative program, sponsored by Prison Fellowship, in a prison in Newton, Iowa.

Rev. Barry W. Lynn of Americans United called the initiative "a government-funded conversion program" and demanded that it be shut down. "It is both unconstitutional and morally wrong for the government to pressure inmates to convert to evangelical Christianity," Lynn said.

Only about 40 percent of the program's budget was taxpayer-funded, and all of that money went to nonreligious purposes.

Inmates have religious freedom, and if they want to explore faith as a way to change their lives so they won't come back to prison, they should be free to do so.

Mark Earley, president and CEO, Prison Fellowship

Prison Fellowship has proven effective in dramatically lowering re-arrest and recidivism rates among inmates who completed voluntary programs in Kansas, Texas, and Iowa. More than two-thirds of the inmates released from American prisons are re-arrested. State prison officials are eager to encourage and support inmate rehabilitation programs, especially ones like Prison Fellowship with a demonstrated record of success.

After five years of legal struggles, Prison Fellowship finally ended its program in Newtown prison when the U.S. Court of Appeals for the Eighth Circuit ruled against the fellowship. Barry Lynn praised the court's ruling, saying that it cast "a very long, very deep shadow over the constitutionality of faith-based state programs."

While Planned Parenthood, the nation's largest abortion mill, can receive millions of tax dollars a year, and the ACLU can get their legal fees for suing the Boy Scouts reimbursed by the taxpayers, Prison Fellowship, which actually helps people, cannot receive any government support.

Americans United writes on its Web site: "Separation of church and state is the only principle that can ensure religious and philosophical freedom for all Americans."

That principle ensures that released and unrehabilitated prisoners will be free to commit more crimes against innocent people. But at least they will not have been exposed to Christianity.

CHAPTER SEVEN

The New Persecutors

The homosexual cause moved naturally from a plea for tolerance to cultural conquest.

–ROBERT R. REILLY, CHAIRMAN,
COMMITTEE FOR WESTERN CIVILIZATION

We can undermine the moral authority of homophobic churches by portraying them as antiquated backwaters, badly out of step with the times and with the latest findings of psychology. Against the mighty pull of institutional religion, one must set the mightier draw of science and public opinion. . . . Such an unholy alliance has worked well against churches before, on such topics as divorce and abortion.

–MARSHALL KIRK AND HUNTER MADSEN, *AFTER THE BALL:
HOW AMERICA WILL CONQUER ITS FEAR AND
HATRED OF GAYS IN THE 90'S*

How Bad Can It Get?

Over the course of my career, some of my best friends and allies have told me, from time to time, that I was exaggerating the dangers we faced. When I condemned *Playboy* magazine and said it would lead to much worse, even some good Christian friends said, "Calm down, Don. People can see more in *National Geographic*." Now we have the most depraved pornography imaginable universally available on the Internet and in most hotel rooms in America, and millions of men, including Christian husbands, are ensnared by it. When I warned that the homosexual movement would push for homosexual marriage, they told me, "Don, you'll lose credibility if you make such exaggerated claims. We're never going to have homosexual marriage." As I write, Connecticut's highest court has ruled that excluding same-sex marriages in that state was unconstitutional. When I warned that sex education programs would become propaganda for teen sex and even sodomy, they said, "Don, remember Chicken Little! Parents will never stand for teaching homosexuality in school."

Now, luckily for them, most of my friends are smarter than I am, so what did they miss? I think it's Newton's first law that says that a body in motion tends to remain in motion, unless of course something stops it. Instead of focusing on where America stood on any one of these issues at any one time, I looked at the direction in which we were traveling. And I think all this time we have been traveling toward two principles, neither of which most people would have said out loud at the beginning, but which now dominate our culture.

The first principle is: "Sex must be separated from married love."

And the second is: "Anyone who dissents from the first principle is a bigot and should be ostracized."

Of course *Playboy* didn't seem important enough to turn an entire society's views on sex and marriage upside down. And it wasn't, all by itself. But that first principle is exactly what Hugh Hefner called the "*Playboy* philosophy," and it showed in which direction we were moving. It was a sign of the times.

And, of course, people like me who criticized *Playboy* back in those days were not called bigots nor were we ostracized. We were just called prudes or old fogies and told to mind our own business. But still, it showed where we were headed.

So how bad can it get? Will there be violence against Christians? Will Christians be forced outside the law where anyone can attack us without fear of justice?

I don't like to believe that it's true. But it's where we are heading logically and as a matter of fact. Christians, particularly evangelical Christians or what the media call the Christian Right, are the most hated people in America today, especially among the elite.

But that's not the worst thing or the most dangerous thing. The most dangerous thing is that the elite are not embarrassed about hating Christians. We are all subject to sins of anger and hatred and bigotry. Any man who denies he has ever felt anger in his heart against someone for being different or for being part of another group is a fool and a hypocrite. But the great danger now is that our new breed of liberal, a person who says his highest value is tolerance, is in the grip of terrible bigotry against Christians. It is the man who does not know he is a bigot, the self-righteous man who has no idea of his own sins who is the greatest danger. The bigot who does not know he is a bigot can justify anything.

Mocking or insulting devout Christians, particularly evangelicals, has become a stock in trade for even so-called "mainstream" entertainers like Garrison Keillor, whose *Prairie Home Companion* radio program often includes gratuitous insults against Christians. It's sad because millions of people in America, maybe tens of millions, including me, have listened to Garrison Keillor's show in the past and have thought it was often both funny and sweet. But it's not so funny and sweet to say, even joke, that millions of your fellow Americans, because they believe in Jesus Christ, should have their right to vote taken away. And it is not at all funny or sweet to have the audience break out into wild applause and laughter. But that's what happened:

I am now the chairman of a national campaign to pass a
constitutional amendment to take the right to vote away

from born-again Christians [enthusiastic audience applause]. Just a little project of mine. My feeling is that born-again people are citizens of heaven, that is where their citizenship is, [audience laughter] in heaven; it's not here among us in America.... If born-again Christians are allowed to vote in this country, then why not Canadians?

Garrison Keillor, *Prairie Home Companion*, November 6, 2004

Ironically, the core of the new liberal bigots' charge against Christians is bigotry. The relentless focus of their efforts is to redefine Christian faith as bigotry because in our society successfully branding someone as a bigot, for all practical purposes, puts that person outside the protection of the law or even outside the circle of civility. The new liberals, through their words and actions, relentlessly teach the message that Christians are intolerant, they are judgmental, they are bigots. And in the liberal catechism, bigots deserve to be hated. Bigots have no rights.

If the elite teaches that message, what do you expect will happen?

The "Philadelphia 11"

Every year the city of Philadelphia has a public celebration of homosexuality called OUTFest where thousands of people gather in a fifteen-block area called the "Gayborhood." For the OUTFest held on October 10, 2004, the city of Philadelphia paid $22,500 of taxpayer dollars to the event's organizers. (Remember, this is the same city that wanted the Boy Scouts to pay $200,000 a year for rent.)

At the center of the OUTFest was a stage where various acts of open lewdness were being conducted. And throughout the "celebration" very disturbing things were taking place in front of children.

That day, eleven members of the Christian group Repent America (RA) attended OUTFest, which is an open, public event. As Christians, they felt there needed to be some kind of response to a public celebration of sin. At first, police officers told the Christians that they were on a public sidewalk on a public street and had as much right as anyone else to be there, or to go wherever they wanted. Conducting themselves in a respectful manner, the Christians entered the event. They banded together and began to sing "Blessed Be the Name of the Lord."

Organizers of the OUTFest event knew in advance that the Christians would be in attendance and formed a group security force called the "Pink Angels" to make sure that the Christians were neither seen nor heard. The Pink Angels linked arms to form human chains and carried large insulation panels to block the Christians from being able to move along the street. They also blew whistles and screamed obscenities at the Christian group, with the apparent intention of annoying and harassing them. Since harassment of this nature is against Pennsylvania law, Michael Marcavage, a member of Repent America, alerted the nearby Philadelphia police officers. Chief Inspector James Tiano, a department liaison to the gay and lesbian community who handles most homosexual public events in Philadelphia, refused to take any action to defend the eleven Christians. Instead, he told Marcavage, "If you feel that way, I think you should seek relief through injunctive relief or through the courts." The Christians were soon told to move to a street corner nearby. For their own safety? No, when they got to the corner, there was a paddy wagon waiting for them.

All eleven members of Repent America were arrested, including two grandmothers and one seventeen-year-old girl. They were held in jail overnight, remaining imprisoned for twenty-one hours before being charged. Each member of the "Philadelphia 11" was charged with three felonies and five misdemeanors. The charges were the following: criminal conspiracy, possession of instruments of crime, reckless endangerment of another person, ethnic intimidation, riot, failure to disperse, disorderly conduct, and obstructing highways. The maximum sentence for these charges totaled forty-seven years in prison and $90,000 in fines.

At the time, Pennsylvania had a law on the books (since rescinded) called the Ethnic Intimidation and Vandalism Act. This is one of a new breed of legislation being enacted at the state level, but also proposed in Washington on the federal level, known as hate crimes laws. The Ethnic Intimidation and Vandalism Act was meant to protect members of ethnic minorities. Then it was amended to include sexual orientation. In effect, it became a crime in Pennsylvania to criticize homosexual behavior.

At the December 2004 preliminary hearing, Assistant District Attorney Charles Ehrlich characterized the protesters' reading Bible verses that condemn homosexual acts as "hateful, disgusting, despicable," and "fighting words."

After the hearing, Judge William Austin Meehan ordered four of the Christians to stand trial on three felony and five misdemeanor charges and dismissed charges against five of them. The seventeen-year-old girl went through the juvenile justice system where the charges were eventually dropped.

Following the hearing, Michael Marcavage received an obscenity-laden message on his phone's answering machine. The caller said he hoped Marcavage would be raped in prison. Thankfully, Judge Pamela Dembe of the Philadelphia County Court of Common Pleas dismissed the criminal charges as being without merit on February 17, 2005.

So again, we might say, "happy ending." But to realize what

an incident like this means we have to think not about where we are but rather where we are heading. I have heard it argued that the Philadelphia 11 were being deliberately provocative. And maybe that's true. But even if it is, there is a long history of protest in this country, and protestors are usually trying to be provocative in order to draw attention to their message. But three felony and five misdemeanor charges? When was the last time some homosexual protest group got slammed with felony charges for singing songs at a public event? If you want to know which way our society is headed, a good test is to answer these questions: Who is allowed to speak out? Who is allowed to protest? Who is allowed to be provocative? And who gets sent to jail for doing the same thing?

> Our critics will say we're bigots who don't want non-Christians to have a voice in society. That's completely untrue. We support every person's right to free speech, even if we disagree with their message. But allowing the freedom to some should not restrict it for others.
>
> Janet Parshall, from the TV series *Speechless*

The persecution of the Philadelphia 11 is part of a larger pattern of harassment and a legal double standard used to keep Christians from expressing their beliefs. Tactics may vary, but the goal is the same—to push Christianity outside the margins of acceptable expression and behavior. And that road ends in one place, silencing all Christians.

Here are some other recent instances of ways Christians have been treated for being "provocative":

- A fireman in Madison, Wisconsin, was suspended from his job and ordered to take diversity training because he gave out flyers describing scriptural teaching on homosexuality. After refusing to take the training, he was fired. *Fired*. Can you imagine such treatment toward a homosexual who was "insensitive" to Christians?

- Shortly after Colorado voters passed a constitutional amendment denying special legal privileges to homosexuals, homosexual activists descended on a church attended by one prominent supporter of the new law. As the service was about to begin, the activists stood up and bombarded the congregation with condoms. This was not on a public street but on private property inside a church. Do you think the homosexual activists were arrested and charged with felonies for being "provocative"?

- On October 29, 2005, a mob of one thousand angry demonstrators attempted to disrupt the "Love Won Out" conference at Boston's Tremont Temple Baptist Church. The conference featured former homosexuals and others who spoke out against homosexual behavior. Despite intimidation and threats of violence from the demonstrators, the police stood by and did nothing.

- On at least two occasions, the San Francisco Police Department has refused to protect Christians against homosexual persecutors, even when the police acknowledged that the homosexuals were breaking the law.

- Two men were arrested in Dayton, Tennessee, on charges of disorderly conduct for attempting to raise wooden crosses on the other side of the freeway where a "Gay Day" event was being held.

We have heard a great deal about gay bashing in recent years, including a few highly publicized cases in which homosexuals were horribly brutalized or murdered for being gay. It is absolutely right that such cases be brought to the public's attention and that police and prosecutors crack down hard against any crime of violence. But most Americans have never heard of the growing wave of violence against Christians, violence incited by the rhetoric of liberals who would never do such things themselves. And the fact that so little is known about these attacks is a sign of where we are headed.

In his book *Christian Bashing*, Dr. Gary Cass documents that this "rhetoric paves the way for behavior. One of the things that I found very shocking is the increase of violence against Christians on church properties. In just a very cursory look online, I found ten instances of church shootings over the last three years. That doesn't get reported, where Christians are being shot in church."

The caricatures that homosexual activists and liberals have painted of Christians created an atmosphere of intolerance where violence is being perpetrated against Christians even in their own churches.

> We live in what most people would consider the most
> tolerant era in history. Yet policies and practices designed
> to make us more inclusive are actually killing free speech
> and the free exercise of religion.
>
> Janet Parshall, from the TV series *Speechless*

San Francisco is one of the most "tolerant" cities in the nation, as the new liberals define "tolerance." In other words, the city has been the scene of shocking displays of hatred and aggression toward Christians, their beliefs, and their institutions.

San Francisco's annual Folsom Street Fair has become little more than a public celebration of homosexuality, sadomasochism, and other perversions. In a poster advertising the September 30, 2007, street fair, a group of radical gay activists called The Sisters of

Perpetual Indulgence (whose motto is "Go forth and sin some more") posed in a blasphemous parody of Leonardo da Vinci's *Last Supper* in which Jesus Christ and his disciples are portrayed as sexual perverts dressed in leather outfits, and the table is littered with obscene sex toys. (Every Easter Sunday, the Sisters of Perpetual Indulgence perform a "Hunky Jesus Contest" in a local park. This is the same city that refuses to allow the Boy Scouts to use its parks.)

When the bishop of the Catholic Archdiocese of San Francisco dared to complain about the poster, the Sisters of Perpetual Indulgence crashed a Roman Catholic worship service on October 7, 2007, desecrated the Eucharist, and mocked the believers, videotaping the event to broadcast it later. Authorities have taken no action against the group, partly because the church seems to have been too intimidated to pursue the matter.

What message did that send to other Christian bashers?

That same week, a man was arrested for trying to set fire to a San Francisco convent where six nuns were sleeping.

Once such acts as sacrilege, blasphemy, vandalism, and arson committed against the church are seen as acceptable, there will be more similar behavior, and it will become increasingly violent and extreme.

"You Christians brought this on yourselves. I'm coming for EVERYONE soon, and I WILL be armed to the @#%$ teeth, and I WILL shoot to kill. God, I can't wait till I can kill you people. Feel no remorse, no sense of shame. I don't care if I live or die." This rant was posted on a Web site by Matthew Murray, twenty-four, of Englewood, Colorado, just before he killed four people in two separate attacks at Youth With A Mission training center for missionaries in Arvada, Colorado, and at New Life Church in Colorado Springs on December 9, 2007.

As Dr. Gary Cass says, "Anti-Christian sentiments are being fomented in the culture and are becoming more deadly and cynical.

Impressionable young people are being swept up in anti-Christian hysteria." This is no surprise when "safe schools" programs like the ones we looked at in chapter three teach students that Christians want to torture those with whom they disagree.

Where does it lead? Where are we heading? Not toward diversity, that's for sure.

CHAPTER EIGHT

The Children of this World

In many regards, the workplace is the leading edge of change for the GLBT [gay, lesbian, bisexual, transgender] community. Company CEOs and executives can often wield more power than state and local officials in creating significant changes that affect their employees' lives. They can enact new policies with the approval of a few board members rather than thousands or even millions of voters.

—NATIONAL GAY AND LESBIAN TASK FORCE:
LESBIAN, GAY, BISEXUAL & TRANSGENDER CAMPUS ORGANIZING: A COMPREHENSIVE MANUAL

[Major Fortune 100 company] aggressively pushes and promotes the homosexual agenda in the name of tolerance, but the minute someone speaks up with what would be considered the traditional moral-values viewpoint, the tolerance disappears and it results in a termination.

—DAVID GIBBS, ATTORNEY FOR TERRY SCHIAVO'S FAMILY AND FOR J. MATT BARBER, FORMER [MAJOR FORTUNE 100 COMPANY] EMPLOYEE

Corporate America has become a major battleground in the culture war and one in which traditional values are consistently losing. The vast power held by corporations, not only in our economic life but also in our society at large, poses many different challenges to traditional Christian morality. Corporations sponsor obscene and pornographic television programs through their advertising. They help establish a materialistic ethos that is contrary to Christian thrift and modesty.

Increasingly, corporations have joined together with homosexual activists to help them pursue their radical agenda. When corporate America endorses and supports homosexual behavior, traditional values don't stand much of a chance. If corporate America's embrace of the homosexual agenda is not stopped, it will be difficult, perhaps impossible, for Christians to prevail in the culture war.

> This is illustrative of what's happening around the country in corporate America. [Major Fortune 100 company] has 'diversity' training that is nothing short of homosexual indoctrination. They make it clear that if you don't accept it as normal, you're a homophobic bigot. Talk about creating a hostile work environment.
>
> J. Matt Barber

Known in Chicago boxing circles as "Bam-Bam," J. Matt Barber is a former professional heavyweight. He worked as a manager in a major Fortune 100 company's corporate security division (one of the conditions in his settlement with his former employer is that he not publicly mention the company's name) in the suburbs of Chicago, Illinois. He also spends his time as a jazz drummer and a Web commentator. The holder of both a law degree and a master's degree in public policy, Barber wrote a column titled "Intolerance Will Not Be Tolerated! The Gay Agenda vs. Family Values," which was published December 17, 2004, on the Web site www.theconservativevoice.com.

Here is an excerpt from his column:

> Many homosexuals choose not to recognize that the majority of their detractors really do care for them as individuals, hold no animus toward them, and would not

presume to dictate what sexual anomalies they entertain behind closed doors, whether self-destructive or not. However, when militant homosexual activists attempt to quell all criticism of their behavior, force society to accept that behavior, and further attempt to alter the fabric of society by changing it to correspond with their own morally relative, androgynous notion of marriage, then those same activists shouldn't be at all surprised to discover that they've angered those who value the sanctity of marriage—they shouldn't be taken aback to find that they have one hell of a fight on their hands—to expect anything less would be queer indeed.

More than a month after the column was originally posted, Barber was summoned to a meeting with two officials from his employer's Human Resource Department. Apparently a "customer" had complained about Barber's column (the customer turned out to be the homosexual activist group Human Rights Campaign). Barber was told: "Here at [major Fortune 100 company] we have a very diverse community," and the views expressed in Barber's column were not consistent with those corporate policies.

[Major Fortune 100 company] financially supports homosexual advocacy groups such as the Gay and Lesbian Alliance Against Defamation and the Lambda Legal Defense and Education Fund. It also provides domestic-partner benefits for same-sex couples and requires employees to undergo diversity training.

Barber explained that the article was a reflection of his Christian beliefs and that he had every right to publish the article. He had written it at home on his own time, without any mention of his affiliation with his employer, or any suggestion that his employer shared his views.

None of that mattered. Barber was suspended without pay and immediately ushered off company grounds in a humiliating fashion after the meeting.

> The basic rights of Christians are hanging in the balance. People just like you and me are being threatened with lawsuits, losing their jobs, and struggling to impart values to their children.
>
> Janet Parshall, from the TV series *Speechless*

Three days later Barber was fired. His wife had just delivered their third child in four years, following a difficult pregnancy that ended in a Caesarean section. His corporate employer took away both his salary and his health insurance at a time when his family was in great need. The company would not extend his family's health insurance while he looked for another job. In addition, his employer refused to provide Barber with a written justification for his termination. As Barber says, "I always knew that people were persecuted in the workplace for their religious beliefs, but I never imagined it would happen to my family and me. We're losing our home, and we may be forced into bankruptcy. But I know that somehow God will provide. I believe it's crucial to take a stand for truth even if that stand results in suffering in the short term."

Barber's case is not unique. All over America, Christians are being disciplined, fined, and even fired from their jobs for various transgressions against political correctness.

- In Cedar Rapids, Iowa, Thomas Meeker, a senior systems engineer for Rockwell Collins, Inc. was fired for refusing to submit to "diversity training."
- Rolf Szabo was fired from Eastman-Kodak for objecting to pro-homosexual memos sent through his employer's e-mail system.

- Christian Richard Peterson was fired from his job at Hewlett-Packard in Boise, Idaho, after twenty-one years, for "insubordination" when he displayed Bible verses critical of homosexual behavior on his desk in reaction to a company-wide pro-homosexual campaign.

- General Motors prohibited an employee from forming a "GM Christian Employee Network" because it was seen as an affinity group based on religion. Meanwhile, other groups based on race, gender, disabilities, and sexual orientation were allowed by the company.

- When Betty Sabatino, trust administrator for Texas Commerce Bank in San Antonio, attended a management-orientation seminar, she was told that sexual orientation would be added to the company's nondiscrimination policy. Since the event was held in a "safe zone," where participants were encouraged to speak up, Sabatino asked why special consideration should be given to people because of their behavior. She was admonished by her boss, recommended for counseling, and eventually fired.

- Christian employees at Sandia National Laboratories in Albuquerque, New Mexico, were ordered to remove postings from the company bulletin board announcing religious events. In turn, any computer screen-savers with religious content had to be deleted. When some homosexual employees complained that it "offended" them to see photos of traditional couples and children in the workplace, married workers were asked not to display family photos to publicize their own personal relationships.

- An evangelical group was told to close all of its accounts because the group did not follow the bank's diversity policies.

One of the reasons why corporate America is so important

in the culture war is that committed and organized activists can effect corporate policy. Homosexual employees insist on antidiscrimination policies and domestic-partner benefits. Radical homosexual organizations ask for direct funding from corporations and threaten boycotts or propaganda campaigns if they don't receive funding. They place openly homosexual men and women on corporate boards. And they solicit official sponsorship of homosexual activities, like parades or sporting events.

More than half of Fortune 500 corporations now offer domestic-partner benefits to their employees. Rep. Barney Frank (D-Mass.), an openly gay legislator, is using the example of corporate America to push for federal domestic-partner legislation. This is yet another example of how homosexual activists seek out the path of least resistance in order to promote their agenda. First they pressure corporations to provide domestic-partner benefits. Then they argue that since corporations are providing these benefits, the government should as well. Finally, domestic-partner benefits are used as an argument for same-sex marriage. Since 86 percent of Fortune 500 companies prohibit discrimination on the basis of sexual orientation, it is not hard to predict the passage of federal legislation in the near future.

Sometimes local political pressure can be brought to bear upon corporations, with ripple effects that spread throughout the country. In 1996, the San Francisco Board of Supervisors passed an ordinance requiring that all companies doing business with the city offer domestic-partner benefits to their employees. (To give you an idea of the financial stakes, the city of San Francisco had a $6.4 billion budget in 2008.) As a result of this policy, thousands of corporations began offering benefits to the domestic partners of their employees. When the ordinance was enacted, one hundred companies offered such benefits. Five years later the number was thirty-two hundred.

Policies like domestic-partner benefits are just the beginning. Corporate diversity programs institutionalize bias against Christian beliefs and undermine traditional values. Brian McNaught is a "diversity guru" who consults for many Fortune 500 companies, including AT&T. He tells employers, "[H]eterosexist language can also be changed. We can say, for instance, 'partner' or 'significant other' rather than 'spouse.' We can say, 'Are you in a relationship?' rather than 'Are you married?'"

Every year, the Human Rights Campaign (HRC) publishes a Corporate Equality Index, which marks how corporations measure up when it comes to indices such as:

- Diversity training
- Nondiscrimination policies including sexual orientation
- Pro-homosexual events
- Advertisements geared toward homosexual customers
- Punishing employees who object to open displays of homosexual behavior in the workplace
- Paying for employees' sex-change operations

Many large corporations gain points by contributing funds to HRC and other homosexual activist organizations. Elizabeth Birch, former president and executive director of HRC, has said that corporate America has become "the driving engine" of homosexual activism.

Why are corporations so eager to follow the homosexual agenda? They think it's good business. As Alan Sears and Craig Osten point out in their book *The Homosexual Agenda*: "[T]he radical homosexual agenda is not about tolerance; it is about acceptance and an in-your-face desire to flaunt homosexuals' sexuality and related behavior at the expense of others. And, as long as their money rolls into the corporate coffers, many corporations seemingly have little or no trouble going along with them."

Shakedown Artists

Homosexuals tend to be well educated, affluent, and politically active. On average, they have much more disposable income than Christian working families. So when push comes to shove, corporate America often sides with homosexuals despite complaints from their more traditionally minded customers. According to Robert Knight of the Culture and Family Institute, who has tracked the activities of homosexual activists for years, "There are active homosexual groups in most major corporations now, and they do a shakedown where they say, 'If you don't promote our events, you're exhibiting bigotry and hatred, and we're going to let everybody know that and . . . it will hurt your sales.'"

Putting the dollar first makes corporate America particularly susceptible to this kind of homosexual blackmail. If a corporation runs afoul of HRC, or any other homosexual group, activists can mount a boycott campaign with lasting consequences to a corporation's brand.

The number of corporations that have financially supported radical homosexual activist groups is staggering. Here is a partial list of the major homosexual groups and their corporate sponsors:

- The National Gay and Lesbian Task Force: American Airlines, Bacardi, Showtime, and Wells Fargo.
- Lambda Legal Defense and Education Fund: Deloitte, IBM, Wells Fargo, Hilton, Microsoft, and Merrill Lynch.
- Human Rights Campaign (HRC): American Airlines, Citibank, IBM, Deloitte, Ernst and Young, Prudential, AT&T, BP, Chase, Harrah's, MGM Mirage, Nike, Showtime, Volvo,

Dell, Merrill Lynch, Price Waterhouse, Shell, UPS, Starwood Hotels and Resorts Worldwide, Washington Mutual Bank.

- Gay and Lesbian Alliance Against Discrimination (GLAAD): Absolut Vodka, IBM, AT&T, Time Warner, MTV, Allstate Insurance, American Airlines, Bud Light, Coors, Comcast, Diet Pepsi, Disney, Goldman Sachs, Hyatt, Lehman Bros., Marriott, Prudential, Quantas, Showtime, Tylenol, Great Britain, and Wyndham hotel group.

In 2003, the chairman of the Progressive Corporation, Peter Lewis, gave $8 million to the ACLU, the largest individual donation the group has ever received. In 1999, the Ford Foundation gave $7 million, which Lewis matched, for a total of $14 million.

Starbucks, in 2005, sponsored a Gay Pride parade in San Diego, including a "youth hangout space" and a "children's garden," an event where two registered pedophiles worked as volunteers and numerous acts of public lewdness were witnessed. At the corporation's home in Seattle, Washington, seventy-five Starbucks employees marched in the parade wearing promotional T-shirts in rainbow colors with "PRIDE" printed on them. A company van followed, with employees passing out coffee samples. Starbucks is also a sponsor of Planned Parenthood.

Homosexual activists began infiltrating Disney entertainment parks with regularly scheduled "Gay Days," attending the parks wearing similar clothing to identify themselves. Sometimes homosexuals took over the parks, flaunting their behavior in front of children. Rather than insisting on standards of decency and decorum in what are meant for children, after all, Disney didn't just allow homosexuals to continue with their objectionable behavior—it encouraged them to come to Disney parks to spend their money. Now Gay Days are regular Disney events.

Numerous corporations, including Nordstrom's, J. Crew, and

Enterprise Rent-A-Car, dropped their affiliation with the online marketing firm kingdomBuy.com when they learned that it contributed to Christian organizations like the AFA.

Cracker Barrel Old Country Store faced a long and well-publicized boycott from homosexuals based on the claim that the restaurant chain discriminated in its hiring policies. When planning to open restaurants in the Northeast, Cracker Barrel added "sexual orientation" to its employee antidiscrimination code and saw its Human Rights Campaign rating improve.

Even with these and other high-profile victories, homosexual activists are not satisfied. The more corporate America gives in to their agenda, the more they demand, and the more Christian organizations and individuals will be forced to keep their beliefs to themselves.

McDonald's Is Their Kind of Place

McDonald's has taken sides in the culture war choosing to continue support of the homosexual agenda. American Family Association wrote McDonald's asking the company to: (a) remove McDonald's name and logo from the National Gay and Lesbian Chamber of Commerce (NGLCC) Web site listing McDonald's as a "Corporate Partner and Organization Ally" of NGLCC and (b) remove the endorsement of NGLCC by Richard Ellis, vice president of Communications for McDonald's USA, from the NGLCC Web site.

McDonald's refused both requests. The fast-food giant donated $20,000 to NGLCC in exchange for a seat on the group's board of directors. The NGLCC lobbies Congress on a wide range of issues including the promotion of homosexual marriage. McDonald's, as a corporate entity, puts the full weight of its corporation behind promoting the homosexual agenda, including same-sex marriage.

In response to AFA's request, Pat Harris, McDonald's global chief diversity officer and vice president of Inclusion & Diversity, stated, "I would like to take this opportunity to reaffirm our position on diversity." Translated: McDonald's will not change its policy of supporting the NGLCC and its promotion of homosexual marriage.

When Richard Ellis, who is openly homosexual, got a seat on the NGLCC board of directors, he was quoted as saying, "I'm thrilled to join the National Gay & Lesbian Chamber of Commerce and ready to go to work. I share the NGLCC's passion for business growth and development within the LGBT community, and I look forward to playing a role in moving these important initiatives forward."

The only value corporate America knows is the bottom line. This makes corporations vulnerable to pressure from radical homosexuals, but they are also vulnerable to pressure from Christians. On July 3, 2008, we at the American Family Association announced a boycott of McDonald's, one of several that we have launched over the years. We asked people to sign a petition against McDonald's, share it with their friends, and tell the manager of their local chain that they would not patronize the restaurant until McDonald's changed its policies.

Just three months later in October 2008, I was able to send this wonderful e-mail to our supporters:

Great news! Because of AFA supporters like you, McDonald's has told the AFA it will remain neutral in the culture war regarding homosexual marriage. AFA is ending the boycott of McDonald's. As you know, AFA called for the boycott in May after McDonald's joined the National Gay and Lesbian Chamber of Commerce (NGLCC).

McDonald's said McDonald's vice president Richard Ellis has resigned his position on the board of NGLCC and that his seat on the board will not be replaced. McDonald's also said that the company has no plans to renew its membership in NGLCC when it expires in December.

In an e-mail to McDonald's franchised owners the company said, "It is our policy to not be involved in political and social issues. McDonald's remains neutral on same-sex marriage or any 'homosexual agenda' as defined by the American Family Association."

We appreciate the decision by McDonald's to no longer support political activity by homosexual activist organizations. You might want to thank your local McDonald's manager.

You see! Christians can fight back and win.

The Vast Wasteland

Television is run by corporate America. Most television channels and all of the major networks are owned by corporations, and corporations supply the advertising dollars that pay for the programming on the air. The decline of television from the wholesome fare of the 1950s and early 1960s to the pornographic idiocy that passes for entertainment these days is a reflection of how corporate America has forsaken moral values.

Television has become such a distorted view of American life that, as columnist Michael Medved writes, "A Martian gathering evidence about American society, simply by monitoring our television, would certainly assume that there were more gay people in America than there are evangelical Christians."

For years I have been campaigning against immorality and obscenity on television. One of my first campaigns was "Turn Off Your Television Week," which I launched with a press release in Memphis, Tennessee, in 1977. The *AFA Journal* regularly reviews television programs so you can avoid obscene or blasphemous programs and watch those with positive themes and without objectionable elements. With each review, the *AFA Journal* lists the national sponsors who bought advertising on the program so you can support or boycott that company's products, as you wish.

When H. J. Heinz Company aired a TV ad featuring a family headed by two men (who kiss at the end of the spot), AFA called for the ad to be pulled off the air. Shortly after our members, along with other concerned Christians, bombarded Heinz corporate headquarters with phone calls, e-mails, and letters, a publicist for Heinz called to inform us that the ad would no longer run.

Some fights we win and some we lose, but all of them are worth fighting. Even though individual homosexuals have more purchasing power and political clout than the average Christian family, there are a lot more of us than there are of them.

According to estimates, there are some 70 million evangelical Christians in America (90 percent of Americans believe in God, and only 8 percent never or rarely attend church). According to the most authoritative recent survey, 2.8 percent of men consider themselves homosexual or bisexual while 1.4 percent of women consider themselves lesbian or bisexual. Only 2 percent of both men and women had sex with a person of the same gender during the past year. That would translate to approximately 6 million active homosexuals in America versus 70 million evangelical Christians.

When 2 percent of the population dictates the moral standards of a nation against the strongly held beliefs of the overwhelming majority, that nation is in real trouble.

Christians must simply speak up. Instead of waiting for homosexuals to impose their values on corporate America, and then fighting back in defense, we Christians need to be on the offensive demanding that corporate America reflect traditional American values in the boardroom, in the workplace, and in the culture at large through advertising, donations, and sponsorship. And if you are discriminated against as a Christian, do what J. Matt Barber did.

Barber, you might recall, is the former employee of a major Fortune 100 company who was fired for being politically incorrect. Well, he fought back and won a settlement with his former employer. Bam-Bam Barber now serves as associate dean of Liberty University School of Law and director of Cultural Affairs for Liberty Counsel. He also has a blog on www.newsbull.com where he posts his commentaries without fear of censorship or retribution.

The homosexual activists might have won the first round in the battle for corporate America. But it's not over yet.

CHAPTER NINE

Whose Birthday Is It, Anyway?

It's just the first six letters in Christmas that make it off bounds. If it was another word, like 'Santamas,' that would be just fine. Well, maybe not because Santa means 'saint,' and some schools say even that's too religious. We have the 'c' word now, and that's 'Christ.' It's taboo.

—JOHN WHITEHEAD, FOUNDER AND PRESIDENT,
THE RUTHERFORD INSTITUTE

In 2003, the New York City public school system established a policy of allowing the display of a Jewish menorah and the Islamic star and crescent, but not a Christian nativity scene during the Christmas season.

"New York school officials have managed to insult just about everybody with their policy," commented Kevin J. Hasson, president of the Becket Fund for Religious Liberty. "They doubly insult Christians, both by banning a crèche in the first place and by arguing, in federal court documents, that the depiction of the birth of Christ does not represent a historical event. They insult Jews by deciding that the only way to allow display of a menorah is to define it as a 'secular' symbol. And just for good measure, they insult Muslims by putting the star and crescent into the same 'secular' category."

The Becket Fund gave New York City public schools its annual Ebenezer Award, a specially designed Christmas stocking filled with lumps of coal, awarded each year to "the person or group responsible for the most ridiculous affront to the Christmas and Hanukkah holidays." Previous winners included Virginia Beach, Virginia, that tried to shut down "Mothers Inc.," a Christian charity that provides Christmas food, toys, clothing, and other items to the needy; the city of Kensington, Maryland, that uninvited Santa Claus from its annual Christmas-tree-lighting ceremony; and the city manager of Eugene, Oregon, who banned Christmas trees from any public space in his city.

"It's not often that public officials come up with a way to insult every major monotheistic religious tradition in America in a single policy declaration, but the endlessly creative bureaucrats at the New York City public school system have pulled it off," Hasson declared. "They had plenty of competition for this year's Ebenezer Award but won it going away."

Ninety-six percent of Americans celebrate Christmas, yet the ACLU and its allies in the secular Left have declared war on the holiday. While Islamic and Kwanzaa symbols are seen as legitimate forms of cultural expression, legitimately displayed in public, and Jewish symbols are sometimes (but not always) allowed, nativity scenes and other Christian symbols are routinely prohibited.

Whether or not you believe that Jesus is the Son of God, His birth and crucifixion are historical facts. The Jewish and Islamic symbols, with as much respect as they deserve, are not any more historic than a Christian cross (and Kwanzaa is an entirely invented tradition).

When asked to explain just what they are doing, the ACLU tries to claim that they are fighting public displays of Christmas in order to protect religious freedom.

As president of the ACLU, I am proud of our steadfast assistance to the many citizens, all over the country, who complain about state-sponsored sectarian symbols—many of whom are deeply religious and celebrate Christmas and

Hanukkah in their homes, churches, and synagogues. . . . Maintaining government neutrality toward religions is at least as essential for the holiness of the religion sphere as it is for the pluralism of the secular state. . . . In short, those who celebrate Christmas and Hanukkah as religious holi-days—holy days—should understand that the ACLU is their ally in seeking to stop the government from con-verting these occasions into commercial carnivals.

Nadine Strossen,
president (1991–2008), ACLU

It's very comforting to know that the deeply religious mem-bers of the ACLU and other secular activists have protected the sacred tradition of Christmas in the following ways:

- Banning red poinsettias from the St. Paul, Minnesota, court-house and city hall because they were regarded as a symbol of Christianity.
- Forcing the city of Pittsburgh to call Christmastime "Sparkle Season."
- Renaming a school play from the classic *How the Grinch Stole Christmas* to *How the Grinch Stole the Holidays*.
- Canceling a school's musical production of *A Penguin Christ-mas* for being too religious despite the fact that the play con-tains no religious characters, only Santa, Rudolph, elves, and some penguins.
- Disciplining two thirteen-year-old girls from school in Rochester, New York, for wearing red and green scarves and saying "Merry Christmas" in a school video.
- Firing a volunteer Santa Claus in Baldwin City, Kansas, be-cause he asked a little girl why we celebrate Christmas, and she answered, "Because it's Jesus' birthday."

- Canceling a New Jersey elementary school's third-grade-class field trip to New York City to see the Broadway play *A Christmas Carol*.

An assistant city attorney from Cincinnati, Ohio, actually filed suit claiming that giving federal employees a holiday off for Christmas violated the Establishment Clause of the First Amendment. Nonsense? The case went all the way to the U.S. Supreme Court, which, by denying certiorari affirmed lower courts' decisions to preserve the holiday.

The war against Christmas reached such absurd proportions that FoxNews.com's radio talk show host John Gibson wrote an entire book about it entitled *The War on Christmas: How the Liberal Plot to Ban the Sacred Christian Holiday Is Worse Than You Thought*. He argued that the battle for Christmas could actually turn into a great victory not only for Christians but also for religious liberty for all Americans. Read Gibson's fiery words:

> The revolution against Christianity has been under way for a few years, and now the counterrevolution is gearing up. Those who would ban Christmas and Christians should not mistake the signs on the horizon. The Christians are coming to retake their place in the public square, and the most natural battleground in this war is Christmas.
>
> John Gibson, radio talk show host,
> *The John Gibson Show*

I think he is 100 percent right, which is why, at the American Family Association, we have fought so hard to keep Christmas a celebration, and, yes, a public celebration of Christ. I might add that Christmas is also a celebration of childbirth and the family. In this way, unlike Hanukkah and Ramadan, it's much more than a sectarian religious holiday. It is, for all mankind of any religion or none, a symbol of the fruitfulness and the glory of married love. No wonder it's so threatening to some.

Christians care about Christmas. You can see this in how we are fighting back.

When Ditsy Carmen Suarez went to the Miami-Dade County Permit and Inspection Center in Miami, Florida, she noticed Jewish and Kwanzaa displays but none for Christmas. She was told that a nativity scene had been disallowed because only privately donated "nonreligious symbols" were permitted. When Suarez offered to donate a nativity display, she was told that it would violate the "separation of church and state."

The American Family Association Center for Law and Policy stepped in. We threatened to seek a federal temporary restraining order, and the center allowed Suarez to put up a nativity display.

Because they are elitists who know that their secular ideology is distasteful to a vast majority of Americans, the ACLU prefers fighting its battles in the courts, or rather using the threat of a court battle to intimidate Christians from defending our rights. The ACLU does not stand up for the Constitution; it wages campaigns of confusion and intimidation to get us to give up our constitutional rights without a fight.

Putting a Chill in Christmas

As a result, people throughout the country, inside and outside the government, now make decisions based on the false belief that any Christmas displays that are religious in nature are unconstitutional. Just take the case of Mrs. Arnold of the Plant City Living Center in Plant City, Florida. In November of 2007, Mrs. Arnold, at the time an eighty-five-year-old grandmother, was looking forward to the annual "Hanging of the Greens and Christmas Party" at the center. A Sunday-school class from a church near the living center hosts the party, and at the very end of the hanging of the greens cere-mony, someone places a little angel atop a Christmas tree. But the Plant City Living Center is federally subsidized housing. So instead of allowing Mrs. Arnold and other residents to celebrate Christmas, the center told her that federal law prohibited her from displaying any religious symbols or words having to do with Christmas.

Mrs. Arnold didn't take this injustice lying down. We at the AFA spread the word about her situation and set up links through our Web site, allowing citizens to express their outrage to the Secretary of Housing and Urban Development (HUD) and to President Bush. We got in touch with both HUD officials and with Steve Edelstein, attorney for the Plant City Living Center. That was on November 8, 2007. On November 9, Mr. Edelstein released the following statement:

"I am pleased to report that the Plant City Living Center's recent newsletter regarding holiday decoration policies has been rescinded. The U.S. Department of Housing and Urban Develop-ment (HUD) guarantees the rights of citizens to display religious symbols in public. We support that guarantee.

"I want to take this opportunity to reiterate to you and to in-form your readers that Plant City Living Center respects the reli-gious beliefs of all of its residents. In furtherance of that policy, Plant City Living Center allows residents to decorate their apart-ments and the exterior areas of their apartments in any manner they choose. To use your recent Action Alert as an example, this policy allows residents to place a small Christmas tree outside their door and to decorate their tree in any way they wish. By the way, Plant City's policy also allows angels to be displayed in com-mon areas."

In 2005, a Wisconsin elementary school attempted to secularize the Christmas hymn, "Silent Night." Its new title? "Cold in the Night."

> Cold in the night
> No one in sight
> Winter winds whirl and bite
> How I wish I were happy and warm
> Safe with my family out of the storm . . .

Quite aside from the anti-Christian bigotry of it all, the new lyrics were downright depressing.

One hundred fifty thousand members of the AFA protested the change, and the school relented. Sadly, they dropped the song altogether rather than sing the original version.

In 2007, the same year, the Glenelg High School's chapter of the Fellowship of Christian Athletes (FCA) in Howard County, Maryland, sponsored an "Operation Christmas Child" project to benefit the children of incarcerated parents at Christmas by collecting toys for the children. As part of the project, students posted signs throughout the school, encouraging other students to help those less fortunate.

The school responded by forcing the students to cover up the word "Christmas" on all of the signs and to replace it with "Holiday," so that the signs would read "Operation Holiday Child."

The AFA responded by sending the FCA chapter one thousand Christmas buttons that said, "Merry Christmas: God's Good News!" With the help of our supporters, church members, and pastors all over the country, we have distributed hundreds of thousands of such buttons and stickers over the years. In 2008, through our "Project Merry Christmas" our buttons and stickers carried the phrase, "It's OK to Say Merry Christmas!"

The War on Christmas, Corporate Style

You might think that corporations, particularly retailers, would like Christmas. It's the time they see their largest sales and profits. Yet many corporations are joining up to fight the secular war against Christmas.

At Gap, Old Navy, and Banana Republic, Christmas hardly exists. For these three companies, all owned by Gap Inc., the only items listed as having anything to do with Christmas were a pair of boxer shorts and a child's sleepwear set. At PetSmart, Christmas doesn't exist at all. Everything is simply for the holidays. I wonder which one they mean.

In 2004, even Macy's, renowned for decades for its Christmas window displays in its New York City store on Broadway and 34th Street, struck the phrase "Merry Christmas" from its decorative banners, substituting "Happy Holidays" and "Season's Greetings." "It's ironic that the setting for the classic Christmas film *Miracle on 34th Street* and the perennial sponsor of the Thanksgiving Day Parade featuring Santa suddenly forgot its history," noted Jared Leland, the Becket Fund's media and legal counsel, "not to mention the reason why the bulk of its customers come flooding in this time of year."

In 2007, thousands of American customers asked Kohl's to include Christmas in its in-store promotions and media advertising. The company promised it would, then ignored that promise. Under the FAQ section of its Web site, Kohl's said Christmas "will be featured in print, TV, and radio throughout the season." When the AFA contacted Kohl's, we were told only that the word "Christmas" would be featured in a half-dozen flyers. It made no mention of using Christmas in radio or TV spots or in-store promotions, as promised. And Christmas trees were called "Holiday trees."

In the fall of 2006, New Line Cinema released *The Nativity Story*, a film version of the story of Mary, Joseph, and the birth of Christ. As part of its advertising campaign, it was one of the sponsors of the Christkindlmarket, an annual festival held in Daley Plaza in Chicago. Christkindl literally means "Christ child." Yet Mayor Richard Daley's Office of Special Events still felt the advertisements for a movie about the birth of the Christ child might be " insensitive to the many people of different faiths who come to enjoy the market."

Sometimes all it takes is just one complaint for a retail company to change its anti-Christmas policies. In 2005, the AFA organized an online petition to boycott Target for avoiding the word "Christmas" in its marketing and advertising during the Christmas season. More than seven hundred thousand people signed the online petition. In response, Target agreed to make ads more specific to the approaching holidays of Christmas and Hanukkah.

When Lowe's started calling Christmas trees "Family trees," it heard from Randy Sharp, the AFA's director of Special Projects. Lowe's responded with an apology and a correction, assuring us that it remains proudly committed to selling Christmas trees, as it has done for more than sixty years.

In 2007, a Mrs. Fields' customer service representative said that the company did not offer Christmas products because it "didn't want to offend anyone." A search on its Web site yielded no Christmas items. The AFA issued an Action Alert stating these facts, and within days Mrs. Fields placed Christmas items for sale on its Web site, using the word "Christmas" in product descriptions. The company also inserted the word "Christmas" into its correspondence with its customers.

Many other stores have ignored Christmas during the season. Best Buy, Staples, Office Max, and Nordstrom's have all banned

Christmas from their retail ads, in-store promotions, or television commercials. Sears, now owned by K-Mart, advertised "Holiday trees" in its circulars. However, following a communication from the AFA, the company now displays "Merry Christmas" signs at the entrance to its stores nationwide.

The battle for Christmas is on. We Christians must fight not only because we can win but also because this particular issue sums up so perfectly what's at stake. Did you notice how many of these corporations use the excuse that mentioning the word "Christmas" might *offend* others? The Chicago mayor's office seems to think that even mentioning a movie about Jesus Christ's birth, a historical fact, could be *offensive*.

What they are really saying is that Christianity is offensive. That Christian speech is inherently impolite. That mentioning Jesus Christ is rude.

Here is a good guideline to follow: people believe what they say and they say what they believe. What we are fighting is an ever more powerful legal and cultural standard which states that any expression of Christian belief is unacceptable in polite company. Jesus would understand that. First you're unacceptable in polite company. Then you're crucified.

We need to win this one for Christmas and for all that it stands for. And we can.

CHAPTER TEN

The IRS Inquisition

Fear of retribution by the IRS is a constant temptation for our pastors to hide the light of the Gospel under a bushel. A free people, whose nation was dedicated to religious liberty at its foundation, should never tolerate such subordination of church to state.

—MICHAEL SCHWARTZ, FORMER VICE PRESIDENT FOR
LEGISLATIVE AFFAIRS AND GOVERNMENTAL RELATIONS,
CONCERNED WOMEN FOR AMERICA, AND CURRENT
CHIEF OF STAFF TO SEN. TOM COBURN (R-OK.)

Religious organizations are exempt from paying taxes because the Founders wanted to insulate churches from political pressure. Today, in much the same manner that the First Amendment is undermined and manipulated to censor Christian expression, tax exemption for churches is being used as a weapon that can threaten any preacher who dares to speak out on moral issues. The new liberals are quite happy to have the Internal Revenue Service intimidate churches that stand up against the homosecularist agenda.

Most of the Founders' core political beliefs arose from their religious faith. With few exceptions, they were devout Christians. Because of their Christian faith, their reading of history, and their experience of religious persecution in Europe, the Founders did not want the federal government to establish an official church or to discriminate against members of any denomination.

Today, the secularists argue that religion has no place in our political life and that religious leaders, particularly those of a conservative bent, have too much influence on politics. On the contrary, many of our current problems are the result of religious leaders abdicating their obligation to speak out.

Separation of Principles and Politics

The assumption that religion should stay out of politics would have seemed absurd to the Founders. Christian churches have a long and honorable history of political involvement in America. The churches in which the Founders worshipped were places where heated political debate, and even revolutionary organizing, took place. The role of the Christian church in advocating for the abolition of slavery and later the civil rights movement is well known. It's only natural for Christians to advocate for what is right and fair. To ask Christians to leave their most important principles behind when the subject of politics is brought up is like asking a football player not to use the muscles he has developed in weight training while he's playing in a game. To many Christians, and particularly to those who hold traditional views, their moral and political philosophies are inseparable.

Today, however, people of faith are increasingly required to keep their church activities from crossing any vague or shifting legal boundaries between acceptable and unacceptable behavior. Pastors censor themselves in the pulpit. Political candidates must be aware of what they say or do while attending church. And church buildings cannot be used for any purposes that might be perceived as political, at least if the politics on display displeases the secularists.

Until 1954, the federal tax exemption for churches and religious organizations took no note of politics. In that year, however, without any congressional hearings, Congress tacked on an unprecedented condition. It amended the Internal Revenue Code to prohibit religious organizations from campaigning on behalf of individual candidates. Churches could still work to influence legislation, but the law specified that such activities must not constitute a substantial part of the church's efforts or budget.

Why this new law? Much of the motivation came from one man's hunger for power. Lyndon B. Johnson, the sponsor of the amendment, was in a close campaign for re-election to the United States Senate. His opponent had been garnering support from anti-communist groups, some of which were church-affiliated. To ensure his own re-election, he led the Congress in imposing severe restrictions on the First Amendment rights of the very groups the Founders thought essential to protect.

Initially, the government and the Internal Revenue Service were hesitant to move strongly against churches, even after the law was changed. Today, as the elite culture grows ever more scornful of the Christian faith, and the secularist propaganda campaign to portray Christians as bigots is ever more successful, the law is increasingly exploited to stifle dissent. The churches singled out for harassment are almost always those that strongly defend traditional Christian teachings on sex, marriage, and family.

IRS investigations are usually prompted by a complaint from partisan opponents of the religious institution said to have crossed the line. For instance, Americans United for Separation of Church and State asked the IRS to revoke the tax-exempt status of an entire Catholic diocese in Colorado Springs because Bishop Michael Sheridan sent a letter to one hundred twenty-five thousand Catholics criticizing abortion, stem-cell research, euthanasia, and same-sex marriage. On every point, the bishop was laying out very clear Catholic doctrine. But because these doctrines went against the secularist political agenda, the secularists wanted them to be regarded as political positions. Americans United did not succeed in this case, but of course the diocese had to fight for its rights. The cost of the effort and the risk required for the diocese to defend its rights is nothing less than a legal penalty for exercising its First Amendment rights. If there is a legal penalty for free speech, then speech is no longer free.

In another case, homosexual activists targeted Canyon Ferry Road Baptist Church in Helena, Montana, for showing congregants a video titled *The Battle for Marriage* and for circulating a petition calling for a state constitutional amendment supporting traditional marriage. A formal complaint, aiming to intimidate the churches into silence, was lodged against the church by a pro-homosexual group, which mailed a letter to the state's Commission of Political Practices calling for an investigation into Canyon Ferry Road Baptist's tax-exempt status. The group sent a copy of the letter to hundreds of other Montana churches, in a clear attempt to intimidate the churches into silence.

> You certainly don't convert your church into a political committee when you speak out in favor of marriage.
>
> Gary McCaleb, senior counsel,
> Alliance Defense Fund

Targets of a Double Standard

Democrats, liberals, pro-abortionists, pacifists, radical Islamists, and even secularists, however, can make overtly political speeches in the pulpit without fear of government reprisal. Left-wing groups do not receive the same level of scrutiny. The vast majority of churches found in contravention of the Internal Revenue Code are conservative. Part of the reason is that most conservative Christians believe in free speech for churches and would never think of sending the IRS after liberal churches, no matter how strange we find the notion of a Christian church endorsing sodomy, abortion, or same-sex marriage. We are automatically victims of a double standard because we refuse to use this tactic. I think we are right to refuse. We should never advocate using the IRS to silence any church.

The double standard, however, is enabled by the ambiguity of the Internal Revenue Code and by capricious means of enforcement. Every election season, the government sends a warning letter to religious institutions, reminding them that "churches . . . cannot endorse any candidates, make donations to their campaigns, engage in fundraising, distribute statements, or become involved in any other activities that may be beneficial or detrimental to any candidate." Preachers are also told that they "cannot make partisan comments . . . at official functions." But the IRS itself says that there is "no bright line test" determining whether a religious institution or preacher has crossed the line. Its guidelines state that any evaluation by the agency will "require the balancing of all the facts and circumstances." This means that the criteria used by the IRS are highly subjective and that the final judgment will be made not by the law, but by some Washington bureaucrat. The more vague a regulation, the more powerful the person who interprets it. The more vague a regulation, the more the bureaucrats are subject to influence from secular liberals trying to shut down religious speech. Americans United for Separation of Church and State and the ACLU target conservative churches, making formal complaints to the IRS. Once the IRS receives such a complaint, the agency is duty-bound to investigate. The more vague the rules, the easier it is to file a plausible complaint. And simply forcing churches to respond is a victory for the secularists.

The bias that many conservative Christian preachers have sensed for some time was confirmed when former IRS commissioner Don Alexander told *Insight* magazine that "there was selective enforcement during the Clinton years, when a church against Clinton was audited and its exemption revoked, [but] Clinton and Gore making speeches from the pulpits . . . has been ignored." In 1998, Americans United for Separation of Church and State issued a press release detailing the complaints it made to the IRS concerning voter guides published by eight different churches. Each one of these churches was conservative and affiliated with the Christian Coalition.

Replacing a Democratic administration with a Republican one has not helped. The IRS continues to grow more aggressive. During the 2004 election, the IRS investigated one hundred thirty-two third-party complaints against religious organizations, nearly half of them churches. Of the forty-seven churches whose cases warranted further investigation, thirty-seven were found to be in violation of federal tax code. Mark Everson, commissioner of the IRS, was fully behind this effort, saying the involvement of religious organizations in politics "has the potential to really grow and have a very bad impact on the integrity of charities and churches." But the fact that some churches are found in violation of a vague and confusing tax code manipulated by their political opponents says very little about the integrity of the churches and a great deal about political manipulation of the law.

IRS Speech Police

Recently, the IRS has gone beyond merely reacting to third-party complaints. Through its "Political Activity Compliance Initiative," the agency has warned approximately fifteen thousand nonprofit organizations, most of which are churches, that they risk audits, fines, or even the loss of their tax-exempt status if they engage in political activities. As part of the initiative, the IRS announced that it would not only investigate third-party complaints but also undertake its own inquiries. This means that IRS agents are now reviewing the content of sermons in order to "prevent violations."

The *Wall Street Journal* has pointed out that, although this initiative is meant to appear nonpartisan, none other than Rev. Barry W. Lynn, executive director of Americans United for the Separation of Church and State, was behind it. As the *Journal's* editorial page noted, "For a man who supports nearly every effort to erect a wall of separation, he seems not to mind sending IRS agents into churches if it keeps ministers out of politics."

The IRS initiative clearly puts that agency in the position of judging the expressions of preachers, turning what should be a tax-collecting agency into religious speech police. Even more terrifying than the prospect of IRS agents sitting in the congregation of churches all across America, monitoring the sermons for code violations, is the very real possibility that they won't even need to, because the chilling effect will be so powerful and pervasive that few preachers will dare speak out on political issues.

It's already happening. Preachers are preventing pro-life organizations from using church facilities not because they are unsympathetic but because they fear an IRS investigation. When campaign volunteers from conservative candidates try to hand out literature in church parking lots, they are often told to leave—again, not for fear of political bias but for fear of an audit. Volunteers who have attempted to collect petition signatures for pro-marriage initiatives have been forced off church grounds for similar reasons.

The only thing worse than a church that is threatened by the state is a church that doesn't threaten the state in any way. Right now, it's the federal government that holds the hammer. The IRS can put any church out of business.

And even when a church wins the legal battle, it loses.

During the 1992 presidential election, the Church at Pierce Creek in Vestal, New York, had its tax-exempt status revoked after Dan Little, its pastor at the time, placed full-page advertisements in the *Washington Times* and *USA Today*. The ads took the form of an open letter, with the headline "Christians Beware," criticizing then-presidential candidate Bill Clinton for his support of abortion, homosexual rights, and condom distribution in public schools and asking how a Christian could in good conscience vote for him.

After a three-year investigation, the IRS revoked the church's tax-exempt status. Four years of legal battles followed, at the end of which the IRS decision remained intact, but the church was allowed to reapply for its tax-exempt status and did not have to pay back taxes.

The legal and financial burdens the church undertook in its own defense were enormous. Not every church faced with these charges can afford to fight back. Other churches watching this highly publicized and expensive battle surely learned the lesson that the government intended: censor yourselves or we will censor you.

In late 2005, Citizens for Responsibility and Ethics in Washington (CREW) and Americans United for the Separation of Church and State accused Focus on the Family and its leader Dr. James Dobson of endorsing candidates for political office. In a ninety-nine-page document, CREW demanded that the IRS conduct an investigation into the various activities of Focus on the Family and asked that the IRS revoke the organization's tax-exempt status, as well as impose any relevant fines or penalties. Americans United for the Separation of Church and State filed a separate document that Dobson said "was full of distortions and outright lies."

As much as organizations like CREW and Americans United for the Separation of Church and State would like to bring Focus on the Family down, the aforementioned statements were designed to accomplish an even more diabolical objective: the silencing of all churches from speaking out on the critical issues of our day. Barry Lynn's statement . . . is simply designed to bully and intimidate unsuspecting churches into silence.

Dr. James Dobson, founder and
chairman, Focus on the Family

Despite the best efforts of Barry Lynn and his allies, the IRS found that Dobson and his organization had stayed well within the law. Once again, this might be regarded as a victory, but the fact that Dobson and his organization had to fight so long and so hard to defend themselves (and that they had to be so careful in the first place) demonstrates the perpetual threat that the Internal Revenue Service can pose to religious institutions.

Under current tax law, churches cannot speak out on the moral qualifications of candidates for public office. In order to stay within the boundaries of the law, ministers have to speak in parable or euphemism. The fact that a minister could not mention Bill Clinton's name when discussing adultery or bearing false witness, while the rest of the culture at large was speaking of little else, is an amazing testimony to how far the secularists have succeeded in silencing us.

Sometimes religious institutions go to absurd lengths in order to stay within the law. Churches can distribute voter guides but only under very strict limits. The guides must include all viable candidates for an office and be neutral and unbiased in all statements about them. The guides cannot make any endorsements or editorial commentary, including grades on the candidates' positions. This is very damaging because grades make voter guides much more useful to voters. Knowing whether a politician voted pro-life 100 percent of the time or 40 percent of the time or whether he or she supported Christian moral principles more often or less often is vital factual information. It is not propaganda; it's simply "doing the math."

Grades are forbidden based on the same IRS reasoning that allows churches to make general statements on moral issues, as long as those statements do not mention specific candidates' stands on those issues. So a pastor cannot legally point out that one candidate voted for abortion, same-sex marriage, and homosexual propaganda in the schools and that his opponent opposed them, even though this is a simple matter of fact.

Who can possibly be helped by such a law other than a politician who wants to silence his critics?

> Since our moral views are so intertwined with our political views, it is difficult to imagine how pastors or priests could be expected to be silent on such matters. It is their business to lead on moral issues, and if we limit their ability to speak on political issues, we necessarily restrict them from influencing society on certain moral issues, not to mention their freedom of speech and religion.
>
> David Limbaugh, author of *Persecution: How Liberals Are Waging War Against Christianity*

According to federal law under IRC section 501(h), a church's tax-exempt status can be threatened if a "substantial part of the activities" of that organization includes "carrying on propaganda, or otherwise attempting, to influence legislation." Once again, the guidelines are vague and are subject to interpretation by the IRS itself. What does "substantial" mean, and is the interpretation the same for every church? Candidates for office in attendance at church are allowed to be introduced to the congregation during a service. They are also allowed to preach, teach, or read scriptures. However, they are not allowed to deliver political speeches, to rally support, or to raise funds. Who draws the line between a sermon and a speech, between teaching a lesson and rallying the disciples?

As Michael Schwartz, former vice president of governmental relations for Concerned Women of America points out, "Why should pastors have to become experts on tax law simply to exercise their ministry? In a free society, government simply should not have the power to punish a church for doing the same things that labor unions, newspapers, and other secular institutions take for granted."

Now I have to take up a delicate issue here. Churches in African American communities are seldom, if ever, investigated for violations of the Internal Revenue Code. I am very glad about that and I hope they never are. But many of those churches are deeply involved in the political life of their communities. If they were held to the same standards as many conservative, predominantly white congregations, they would lose their tax-exempt status. Why aren't they held to the same standards? I think the answer is clear. Although most churches in the African American community hold to Christian family principles, for historical reasons many are so firmly committed to the Democratic Party that they form an essential part of that party's infrastructure. Despite African Americans being conservative on many social issues, their churches get a pass from the same liberals who go after other conservative churches.

In 2003, Rep. Walter Jones (R–N.C.) introduced the Houses of Worship Political Speech Protection Act that would have prevented the IRS from revoking the tax-exempt status of religious organizations involved in political activities. The legislation was defeated by a vote of 178 for and 239 against. Every member of the Black Caucus of the House of Representatives voted against the measure in 2003, though many of them frequently speak at churches in their constituencies.

Even if we disagree with the politics of the Black Caucus, conservative Christians should not want the voices of any religious groups to be silenced. No matter how unfairly the IRS picks on conservative churches, I will never, ever support those same laws being used against any church, no matter what the politics of the congregation or the minister. Instead, the Houses of Worship Political Speech Protection Act should be re-introduced and supported by Christians all across America, Left and Right, black and white, to protect our houses of worship from political pressure.

The Founders thought it was not only right and proper but also essential for pastors to speak out against evil, even if politicians were doing the evil. Naturally, politicians don't like this; they never have. Our Lord was crucified by a politician's order. Most of the apostles were martyred on politicians' orders. Happily, no one is threatening to crucify us. All the more reason we should not let ourselves be silenced.

CHAPTER ELEVEN

The UnFairness Doctrine

Conservative radio is a huge threat and political advantage for Republicans, and we have had to find a way to limit it.

—Senior Democratic congressional staffer

One of the advantages of having a strict moral code, a black-and-white account of what's right and wrong (the kind liberals call intolerant or judgmental), is that it teaches us about temptation and conscience. Since Christians know from the Bible what is right and wrong, and since we all know that sometimes we do wrong, we realize that just "knowing" isn't enough. We all share St. Paul's problem: "For the good that I would, I do not, but the evil which I would not, that I practice." We succumb to temptation. And often we do so by clouding our consciences, by denying to ourselves that we are doing wrong.

The advantage a Christian has is that he believes in moral absolutes, which makes it a little harder to deceive one's own conscience. If right and wrong are written down in black and white, it's a lot harder to pretend that stealing or breaking a vow or lying is OK when *we* do it. (We seem to manage it all too often anyway.) That's just one of many ways in which we have it a lot easier than the secularists.

Now no man can judge another's conscience, so I want to be very careful here. But it seems to me, from the outside looking in, that one of the greatest dangers to our country right now is that the new sort of liberals, the secular liberals, are letting their own consciences be clouded by what used to be their foremost principle.

In days past, if I asked a liberal, "What is the number one principle of liberalism?" most of the time he would say, "Free speech." It was as if liberals had their own version of the Great Commandments: "Thou shall love freedom of speech with all thy heart, soul, and mind, and thou shall protect thy neighbor's free speech as thine own." But now liberals are being terribly tempted to go against their most revered principle. Maybe the problem is that they never expected protecting free speech to require a sacrifice, never expected it to mean that they had to give up something they really wanted. Maybe they never really thought about how hard it might be to put up with those they disagree with, speaking up loud and clear in public and even on the air-waves. Anyway, in recent years, they have discovered that free speech isn't free—for them. And as a result, they are being tempted and tested. For America's sake, and theirs, let's hope they pass the test.

Here is what I mean. In our country, for reasons I can't claim to fully understand, Americans whose profession mostly consists of working with words seem to hold different views from Americans whose work has mostly to do with taking action or making things or running a business. Not always, but on average. Most college professors vote Democrat, but professors teaching medicine or finance or accounting are more likely than most other professors to vote Republican or to describe themselves as conservatives. Most journalists, especially at the big national newspapers and the leading networks, vote Democrat. Small businessmen are more likely than reporters or professors to vote Republican. It seems to me at least that city people, who tend to be more liberal, talk a lot more than country people, who tend to be more conservative.

So it is not that surprising that for decades the big national media were dominated by liberals. Liberals never like to admit this, but there are so much polling data and other research to back this up that it is just not possible to deny it. An overwhelming majority of reporters, on the order of 70 and 80 percent or more, depending on which research you look at, vote Democrat and hold liberal positions on issues like abortion or homosexuality.

But starting in the late 1980s, one very big exception to this rule developed. Political talk radio became a huge phenomenon, gaining tens of millions of listeners and callers. And the overwhelming majority of the hosts and of the listeners were conservatives or Christians or both.

What happened to cause this? Part of the explanation is that in 1987 a rule called the Fairness Doctrine that used to make it very difficult for broadcasters to allow controversial opinion shows on the air was finally repealed after several years of being much less strictly enforced.

A "Chilling Effect"

The original intent of the Fairness Doctrine actually was to encourage controversial debate. But it backfired and made most broadcasters back away from controversy of any kind. As James Gattuso, senior research fellow of regulatory policy for the Heritage Foundation explains, "The Fairness Doctrine required broadcasters to . . . provide both or all sides whenever they discuss a controversial issue." But who can say what "both" or "all" sides of an issue are? Broadcasters who guessed wrong could be sued for failing to represent some group's view. Says Gattuso, the Fairness Doctrine in practice "discouraged broadcasters from providing any discussion at all because if you're a station manager and you discuss anything of controversy, someone could sue you."

Broadcasters were not just afraid of citizens suing. They also had very good reason to fear that incumbent politicians, especially whatever party held the White House, would use the Fairness Doctrine as an excuse to shut down critics, while letting their supporters have free reign on the airwaves. They were not imagining this. Several presidents from both parties tried with some success to do just that. John F. Kennedy's assistant secretary of Commerce, Bill Ruder, admitted, "Our massive strategy was to use the Fairness Doctrine to challenge and harass right-wing broadcasters and hope the challenges would be so costly to them that they would be inhibited and decide it was too expensive to continue."

In the 1964 presidential election, the Christian broadcasting station WGCB (Word of God and Christ in the Bible) in Red Lion, Pennsylvania, broadcast an attack against Democratic presidential candidate Lyndon B. Johnson and in favor of Republican presidential candidate Barry Goldwater. The broadcast garnered a Fairness Doctrine complaint as part of a conscious effort by the Democratic Party to silence its opposition. The challenge was taken all the way to the U.S. Supreme Court that found the Fairness Doctrine to be constitutional but that if it proved to restrain free speech, the law's constitutionality would be reconsidered.

President Richard Nixon, who was driven from office for trying to cover up a scheme to spy on his political opponents, used the Fairness Doctrine in a similar fashion against liberal broadcasters.

The Fairness Doctrine resulted in very few fines. The government didn't need to enforce the regulation because it had been so effective in deterring broadcasters from covering any issue that might smack of controversy. Station owners censored themselves because they were afraid of investigations and fines that could have resulted if they found themselves on the wrong side of this law, which, like the Internal Revenue Code on tax-exempt status, was vaguely written and often unfairly applied. When people are so afraid of government that they censor themselves, it's called a "chilling effect." The courts have long recognized the chilling effect as an illegal tactic the government can use to suppress free speech while appearing to take no action.

You might ask, "If the Fairness Doctrine is so opposed to a fundamental American principle like free speech, how could anyone ever have supported it?" The idea back in 1949, when the Federal Communications Commission (FCC) first established the doctrine, was that the frequencies over which radio stations and especially TV stations could broadcast were narrow and scarce. The FCC feared that if the government didn't control how the airwaves were used then some large corporation with a particular point of view might achieve a monopoly. It was really television that prompted this fear because broadcasting images requires a bigger slice of the airwaves than just broadcasting sound on radio.

By the 1980s, after nearly forty years of the Fairness Doctrine, this argument did not really hold up any longer. With FM radio, UHF, and cable television, the airwaves were no longer scarce. The Supreme Court began to question the constitutionality of the doctrine. Meanwhile, the Reagan administration decided that the Fairness Doctrine was obsolete, unnecessary, and counterproductive. In 1987, the Fairness Doctrine was rescinded by a unanimous vote of the FCC commissioners. The Supreme Court eventually upheld that order.

Then came the surprise. As the Fairness Doctrine first fell into disuse under President Reagan and then was finally repealed, many conservatives thought that the result would be a media that would be even more liberal. They feared that without regulation favoring balance, the scales would tip even further toward the Left.

Those worries proved to be dead wrong.

As soon as the Fairness Doctrine was taken off the books, a new industry was born. American radio talk show host and conservative commentator Rush Limbaugh began broadcasting his radio program nationally in August 1988, shortly after the Fairness Doctrine was abolished. Dozens, then hundreds of conservative radio talk show hosts followed in his footsteps, enjoying their new freedom to air their views not only on issues like taxes and government spending but also on abortion and traditional family values. Since churchgoing Christians overwhelmingly are on the "conservative" side of these values issues, liberating conservatives on the radio meant liberating Christians, too, like Janet Parshall and Dr. James Dobson, radio talk show hosts and commentators, who have been lions on our side. These new voices attracted a huge following. Tens of millions of Americans listen to conservative and Christian radio.

Air America Goes Bust

So that was one surprise. But then came the next. The liberal version of talk radio never really caught on. There are some out there, of course, but the liberal voices just did not capture the radio audience the way conservative and Christian voices did. Liberal ventures like *Air America* found themselves facing bankruptcy while conservative programs were raking in both ratings and sponsors. Meanwhile, the polling data still show that the "old media," what we now call "the mainstream media," are still overwhelmingly staffed and managed by liberal Democrats.

I can't say that I know why conservatives took to radio and liberals continue to dominate network TV, any more than I can really be sure why more journalists than brain surgeons vote Democrat. But there it is. Once President Reagan restored freedom of speech to the airwaves, conservative and Christian radio took off, and liberal radio did not. A survey conducted by a liberal group in the spring of 2007 found that of the top-five news/talk commercial radio stations, 91 percent of the weekly political talk radio programming was conservative in outlook. While that figure might be exaggerated by the group's own political perspective, it does show that conservatives and Christians have found a place in the marketplace of ideas.

Reinstating an UnFair Doctrine

And now liberals, or some liberals anyway, want to shut us down. Some liberals are so enraged by talk radio that they are giving in to the temptation to betray their own most strongly held principles. They are trying to bring back the Fairness Doctrine, or something like it under a different name, for one reason and one reason only—to silence the voice of conservative and Christian commentators. And this time they may win.

Members of Congress are especially hostile to talk radio. Congressmen depend on the fact that many of their constituents don't pay much attention to what they do. You can tell this when you see how few Americans turn out to vote on the "off years" when only members of Congress, not the president, are elected. Members of Congress like to "fly beneath the radar," and they hate it when a local talk show host exposes their record to the voters.

Twice before, Congress has voted to reinstate the Fairness Doctrine. In 1987, President Reagan vetoed a bill passed by Congress shortly after the law had been rescinded. Another congressional attempt in 1991 was thwarted when President George Herbert Walker Bush threatened a veto.

This time around the liberals think they can get away with it, probably by disguising their proposals as something that looks quite different from the Fairness Doctrine.

The study I mentioned before, the one that concluded that 91 percent of talk radio is conservative, was called "Structural Imbalance in Political Talk Radio" and conducted by the liberal Center for American Progress and Free Press. The study concluded that the reason conservative voices dominate talk radio is that most radio stations are owned by corporations rather than locals. But this doesn't make any sense at all because it does not explain why so many people listen. It's like saying that tens of millions of people watch Oprah because the stations that broadcast her show are owned by corporations. That's ridiculous. Tens of millions of people watch Oprah because they like Oprah! These corporations aren't charities. If people didn't want conservative and Christian radio, they wouldn't listen and the corporations would go broke. If liberals want to blame someone for talk radio, they should be honest and blame the listeners.

The study proposed elaborate new regulation or re-regulation of radio, specifically: restoring local and national caps on the ownership of commercial radio stations; limiting radio broadcasting licenses to three years; requiring stations to document how they are operating "on behalf of the public interest"; and charging "user fees" to stations that are "unwilling to abide by these regulatory standards." These fees would be paid to the Corporation for Public Broadcasting.

Some of this may sound fine, as if it would really be giving control to communities. But experience shows that all of these rules would mean just one thing: politicians and liberal activists would be able to strong-arm their critics into silence.

You may ask, "What is the problem with requiring 'balance?'" There are two. The first problem is that it will be the politicians who decide what's balanced. The officials who are supposed to be serving the voters will get to rule on what the voters can say about them. (That's sounds great. Can I make a law about what my critics can say about me?)

The second problem is one everyone in the broadcasting business knows: if a broadcaster wants to attract enough of an audience to be profitable and stay on the air, he has to offer consistent programming. Audiences have to know that if they want comedy, they can turn to this station at this hour, or if they want family programming, they can turn to another station. If they want rock and roll, they turn the dial here, or if they want country, they tune the dial there. But a new Fairness Doctrine could require radio stations that run Rush Limbaugh's program to also run a program by, say, Al Franken. It is not inconceivable that Christian broadcasting would have to be "balanced" by homosexuals or even Satanists. If broadcasters can't control their own programming, they won't be able to hold an audience, and talk radio will go out of business.

Talk radio matters. And that is what has really enraged some liberals. In 2007, President Bush, Sen. John McCain, and Sen. Ted Kennedy tried to pass an immigration bill that would have provided amnesty for millions of illegal immigrants. Now whatever you think of that legislation, and many Christians favored it, the main reason it failed was because conservatives made their voices heard on radio. Radio show hosts like Rush Limbaugh got their audiences mobilized to fight against the bill.

That's how a free society works. Arguments are settled in the marketplace of ideas. When the immigration bill was discussed by conservative broadcasters, they brought up points that listeners would not have heard from those who were pushing the bill. And the outcry was massive.

I am not saying that there was not a case to be made for the bill. But the American way is to get out and make your case. Win people to your side; don't shut them up; don't silence them.

The defeat of the immigration bill really should have persuaded the true liberals to defend talk radio because it proved that talk radio is an important part of free speech in this country. But it only made some liberals more committed to clamping down on conservative talk shows. Nancy Pelosi told the *Christian Science Monitor* that she favored a return of the Fairness Doctrine. A senior advisor to the House majority leader told the *American Spectator*: "[Democrats] failed on the radio airwaves with *Air America*, no one wanted to listen. Conservative radio is a huge threat and political advantage for Republicans, and we have had to find a way to limit it." Another aide to Democratic leadership told the *Spectator* that Pelosi was trying to bring down Rush Limbaugh.

"It's time to reinstitute the Fairness Doctrine," said Democratic senator Richard Durbin of Illinois. In a statement typical of liberal elitism masquerading as populism, Durbin went on to say, "The airwaves belong to the American people. Those who profit from them do [so] by permission of the people through their government." But make no mistake about it. If Durbin gets his way, it is the government that will make the call.

Two-time Democratic presidential candidate Dennis Kucinich of Ohio has asked his staff to investigate Salem Radio Network, a national satellite radio network that is Christian-formatted with general news/talk show programming that features conservative broadcasters like Bill Bennett and Michael Medved and Christian hosts such as Dr. Richard Land. "They are identifying senior employees, their political activities, and their political giving," a government reform committee staffer told the *Spectator*. "Salem is a big target, but the big one is going to be Limbaugh. We know we can't shut him up, but we want to make life a bit more difficult for him."

For now, legislative efforts to reinstate the Fairness Doctrine have all been defeated. But the enemies of free speech do not need a congressional majority to get their way in order to put such restrictive measures into law. All they need is control of a few key congressional committees to exercise a tremendous chilling effect. Even if the investigations of Rush Limbaugh and the Salem Network go nowhere, other conservative and Christian broadcasters will be on notice. Those who lack the resources to defend themselves might think twice about speaking out.

Even without direct congressional action, the threat remains. Under current law, the president could restore the Fairness Doctrine with a stroke of his pen. Or the unelected Federal Communications Commission could succumb to pressure from a liberal congress or president to re-impose the same limits with regulations that many citizens would likely never even hear about.

The rationale behind the Fairness Doctrine is utterly obsolete. Today, with cable television, satellite radio, and, of course, the Internet, there is no limit to how many voices can be heard through various communications media. The airwaves are not scarce but abundant. Now there are some fourteen thousand radio stations, twice as many as existed in 1970. Satellite radio did not even exist in the twentieth century. Now it has more than thirteen million subscribers. Eighty-six percent of American households have either cable or satellite television, providing more than five hundred different channels. There are more magazines than there were twenty years ago. The only media in decline is the newspaper industry.

Since deregulation, not only has diversity flourished but media ownership is much more widespread. According to *City Journal*, "[a] 2002 FCC survey of ten media markets—from the largest (New York City) to the smallest (Altoona, Pennsylvania)—showed that each had more outlets and owners in 2000 than in 1960. And the FCC counted all of a market's cable channels as a single outlet (even though the typical viewer would regard each channel as a distinct one) and didn't include national newspapers or Internet sites as media sources, so the diversity picture was even brighter than it seemed."

The scriptures teach us "we haven't been given a spirit of fear, but of power, and of love, and of a sound mind." But looking at the threat posed to our liberties by a restored Fairness Doctrine can be pretty frightening. Without recourse to a vote, the president, or even just an unelected FCC commissioner, could drive conservatives and Christians off the air, as one more step in the new liberals' relentless campaign to drive Christian principles from public life.

CHAPTER TWELVE

The ENDA Agenda

We are creating a civil right.

—FORMER MEMBER OF SAN FRANCISCO'S BOARD
OF SUPERVISORS TERENCE HALLINAN ON THE CITY'S
PASSAGE OF A TRANSGENDER ANTIDISCRIMINATION LAW

Crystal Dixon worked as associate vice president of the Human Resources Department at the University of Toledo in Ohio. On April 4, 2008, Michael Miller, the editor-in-chief of the *Toledo Free Press* published a column titled "Gay Rights and Wrongs." In the article, Miller compared the campaign for same-sex marriage with black people's struggle for civil rights.

Dixon wrote a response to Miller's article, which was published in the newspaper. Under the headline, "Gay Rights and Wrongs: Another Perspective," her piece argued:

[H]uman beings, regardless of their choices in life, are of ultimate value to God and should be viewed the same by others. At the same time, one's personal choices lead to outcomes either positive or negative.

I take great umbrage at the notion that those choosing the homosexual lifestyle are 'civil rights victims.' Here's why. I cannot wake up tomorrow and not be a black woman. I am genetically and biologically a black woman and very pleased to be so as my Creator intended.

Dixon went on to describe how many people were leaving the homosexual lifestyle, aided by religious organizations like Parents and Friends of ExGays and Gays (PFOX) and Exodus International. She also made the point that homosexuals enjoy an elite status in our society, with homosexual men earning an average of $62,000 annually, and lesbians not far behind with $52,000—both figures well ahead of the median income of a non-college-educated black male at $30,539.

And Dixon spoke directly to a point made in Miller's article that homosexual employees at the University of Toledo suffered a disparity in benefits compared to heterosexuals. Dixon explained how Miller's argument was based on a misunderstanding of the university's administrative policies following a merger with the former Medical University of Ohio (which was Dixon's original employer) and how she and her colleagues were working hard to develop a benefits plan that would be fair to all employees. Finally, Dixon expressed her deeply held Christian belief in a Divine order and the consequences of making choices that violate that order.

The day Dixon's article appeared she was placed on "administrative leave." In other words, she was suspended from her job. Shortly after her suspension, Dixon was fired. Dr. Lloyd A. Jacobs, president of the University of Toledo, wrote a letter to Dixon stating that her opinions had resulted in a "loss of confidence in you as an administrator." Dixon responded that she had never discriminated against homosexuals and in fact had hired homosexuals and had recommended the hiring of both homosexuals and heterosexuals based on their qualifications not their sexual orientation.

"Whether or not you agree with me or not is not the issue," Dixon said at a press conference following her dismissal. "The real issue is that I, like every citizen in the United States, have a First Amendment right to exercise free speech and to express my religion."

Even the ACLU came to Dixon's defense—well, sort of. Christine Link, executive director of the ACLU of Ohio, said the focus should be on Dixon's work performance not on her words. But Dixon had to ask the Thomas More Law Center for legal representation in her case against the university.

In yet another *Free Press* article commenting on the matter, Dr. Jacobs wrote: "The University of Toledo welcomes, supports, and places value upon persons of every variety. Disability, race, age, or sexual orientation are not included in any decision-making process nor the evaluation of worth of any individual at this university. To the extent that appearances may exist that are contrary to this value statement, we will continue to do everything in our power to align all of our actions every day with the value system discussed."

Of course in her original letter, Crystal Dixon said almost exactly the same thing about valuing all people equally, and there was never any question about her discriminating against any employee or applicant. Lloyd Jacobs's letter came down to saying that Crystal was fired—or lost her livelihood—because some people might assume that her religious views made her a bigot. That's where we are today. Christian views are presumed to be evidence of bigotry.

Here is what the Family Research Council had to say: "In one fell swoop, Jacobs was informing the world not only that the University of Toledo denies its employees a private right of free speech but that an African American employee has no right to assert her opinion regarding her own civil rights heritage."

Discrimination and Sexual Orientation

The story of Crystal Dixon illustrates a fundamental problem with the homosexual agenda: an elite is claiming discrimination, and the people who really suffer discrimination don't like it.

Unfortunately, homosexual activists are getting sexual orientation added to civil rights laws throughout the nation. Twenty states, the District of Columbia, and one hundred forty city and county governments have passed laws that ban discrimination on the basis of sexual orientation, gender identity, and even "perceived" sexual orientation or gender identity.

The Employment Non-Discrimination Act (ENDA) is a federal bill that would force these same changes on every state in the nation. Not only would employers be free to discipline or fire Christian employees like Crystal Dixon for speaking their minds, they might even be required to. ENDA is nothing more than a weapon being handed to homosecularists to use against Christians to silence and marginalize them.

These antidiscrimination laws are forcing Christians not only to accept but also to participate in behavior they consider sinful. Churches are being told to perform same-sex marriages. Doctors are being successfully sued for not performing artificial insemination to lesbians, even when they offer patients referrals to other doctors. Psychologists are being compelled to offer advice contrary to their own beliefs and opinions. A licensed counselor was fired after she referred a homosexual client to a colleague because the counselor said that meeting the client's needs would conflict with her sincerely held religious beliefs.

On April 18, 2006, Tim Bono, a video technician and small-business owner in Arlington, Virginia, was ordered by the Arlington County Human Rights Commission to duplicate two pro-homosexual videos made by a lesbian activist. Lilli Vincenz had e-mailed Bono, owner of Bono Film and Video, and asked him to duplicate two gay-themed films titled *Gay and Proud* and *Second Largest Minority*. Bono refused the job, stating that it was his company's policy not to duplicate videos that were obscene, that might embarrass his employees, that would damage the company's reputation, or that were against the company's Christian values.

Vincenz complained to the Human Rights Commission, which then ordered Bono to copy the videos. If Bono continued to refuse, the commission would seek to file a discrimination complaint in Arlington Circuit Court.

The basis for such a complaint would be that Bono discriminated against Vincenz because of her sexual orientation. But Bono did not refuse to provide services to homosexuals. He just didn't want to duplicate material that was obviously homosexual propaganda.

An important point needs to be made here. The Bible does not forbid orientation or temptation; it forbids sin. Homosexuality is an orientation or temptation, and sodomy is the sin. For someone to define himself by his temptation is to immediately and irrevocably place that temptation beyond the range of moral criticism. Jesus taught the same lesson for every sin. We must speak out against sin, but we have no right to judge the sinner. If speaking out against the sin is considered the same as judging the sinner, then we can't speak out against lying, stealing, or adultery either, because then we would be judging those who committed those sins.

But that is exactly what the homosecularists are attempting to do. They want to imply that Christians saying that sodomy is a sin or believing that the gay lifestyle is destructive is equivalent to discriminating against homosexuals. By turning opinion into the legal equivalent of discrimination, homosecularists hope to make Christian opinion illegal. If they succeed, they can achieve the complete alteration of American society to fit the homosexual view of human sexuality, marriage, and family.

As Concerned Women for America explains, ENDA "seeks to chill and suppress religious expression and freedom of speech by using the law to transform or extinguish religious practices that are disfavored by the elite . . ."

Under ENDA legislation as it is currently written, religious organizations and businesses with fifteen or fewer employees would be exempt from its provisions, but these exemptions are so vague and problematic that they would probably offer little protection from the inevitable litigation. While schools that are owned by or directed toward a particular religion are exempted, other schools that emphasize religious principles more broadly but do not a have formal religious affiliation would be unprotected. Small businesses that provide services or sell goods to the public would probably be unprotected. That means Christian bookstores, Bible publishers, and others whose businesses it is to disseminate the Gospel will find themselves in court.

And similar legislation in California also had religious exemptions, which were gradually stripped away.

The law would unleash a torrent of litigation, with one possible outcome being the legalization of same-sex marriage throughout America. If discrimination on the basis of sexual orientation or even its perception were made illegal on a federal level, then same-sex couples could claim that they were being discriminated against by not being allowed to marry. The Defense of Marriage Act defines marriage as the legal union between one man and one woman. ENDA could erase that law from the books.

Here are just a few examples of what ENDA would mean in practical terms.

- Declare traditional morality a form of "discrimination" and legally undermine marriage and the family.
- Expand federal powers over the workplace, creating a new way for the government to control business owners and for employees to sue their employers.

- Expose private organizations like the Boy Scouts to federal civil rights litigation for its refusal to give homosexuals leadership positions. (When running for president in 2000, Al Gore told a national television audience that one reason he supported ENDA was that it would force the Boy Scouts to change its policy on leadership positions for homosexuals who are open about their sexuality.)
- Discard all protections for religious expression of employers, freedom of association, or standards for employee behavior, expression, and appearance.
- Create affirmative action programs and other preferential treatment for homosexuals.
- Transform sexual behavior into a legally protected right, with the consequence of forcing the government to condone promiscuous and perverse behavior in the workplace and other public places.
- Elevate multiple-sex-partner relationships into a federally protected right. By including bisexuality in the definition of sexual orientation, the government would officially condone not only homosexuality but also adultery and promiscuity, creating a legal precedent for abolishing any restrictions on polygamy and bigamy.
- Provoke an avalanche of civil rights lawsuits, including statistical analyses of hiring patterns as currently used to prove discrimination against women and ethnic minorities.
- Prohibit employers from considering deviant sexual histories in hiring practices, even for schools and child-care organizations.
- Create legal authority to judge one person by another person's perception of another. After all, that was exactly what was done to Crystal Dixon. The president of the University of Toledo said his policy was to root out any "appearance" of

bigotry. In other words, the first step was taken toward "thought crimes."

- Criminalize any criticism of homosexual behavior or any other sexual deviancy.
- Turn words like "husband" and "wife" into hate speech.
- Make certain passages of the Bible illegal and subject to censorship.

ENDA's Guide to Gender

I realize this is another issue that even my good friends will say I am exaggerating. Well, I may be extrapolating, but I am not exaggerating. Extrapolating simply means looking ahead down the road you're traveling on in order to see where you'll end up. To see down the ENDA road, you have to look at the record and know how the game is played. Liberals in Congress know that the consequences I have sketched out would be intensely unpopular, so they do not write every detail into a bill. All Congress needs to do is give liberal activists and legal groups something to work with in court, a new angle or argument to put before elitist judges. They know that most judges in this country, even when they might be Republican or "conservative" on some issues like government spending, are very liberal on moral issues. ENDA will hand these judges the ball, as it has done so many times before, and the judges will gladly grab it and run with it, while Congress sits on the sidelines looking innocent claiming, "We never voted for that."

In some versions of ENDA, and in laws already on the books in several states and municipalities, transgenderism (cross-dressing, sex change, and other varieties of gender confusion) and perception of sexual orientation are given full protection as civil rights.

How might that affect you? Say you owned a business large

enough to have male and female restrooms. One day, a male employee tells you that he is transgendered. Sometimes he feels like a man; sometimes he feels like a woman; and sometimes he just isn't sure. He could come to work dressed as a man one day, a woman the next, or even change during his lunch hour. He could wear any kind of clothing, jewelry, or piercings he felt like wearing. He could talk about his sexual adventures or fantasies without fear of penalty or disapproval. He could use the men's room or the ladies' room, depending on what gender he felt he was at the time. And if you criticized, disciplined, asked him to make up his mind, or fired him, you'd be in violation of the law.

Protecting perceived sexual orientation or gender means that an employee who isn't actually homosexual, but claims that you perceive him as such, would be able to take you to court for violating his civil rights. Even the most innocuous statements could incur legal damages, and employees fired for good cause could claim they were actually fired because of their employer's perception of their sexual orientation or gender identity.

According to California state law, "'gender' means sex and includes a person's gender identity and gender-related appearance and behavior whether or not stereotypically associated with the person's assigned sex at birth." Under this definition, gender means nothing at all. Laws like California's will undermine and eventually eliminate any distinction between man and woman.

Current civil rights laws prohibit workplace discrimination on the basis of race, sex, religion, or handicap. ENDA would effectively knock off religion from the protected list for Christians and would also make it much more difficult to enforce rules forbidding "hostile work environments" for women. Right now, and justly so, a male employee who behaves lewdly or posts pornographic pictures or a "girly" pin-up calendar in his workplace must be disciplined, or the employer can be sued by women who are made to feel uncomfortable. But if gender is a protected status, and gender is a matter of perception, then how can the expression of gender be illegal?

Remember, according to the American Psychiatric Association, there are at least twenty different sexual orientations. Actually practicing some of these orientations (like pedophilia) is illegal. With ENDA, suddenly these orientations would be fully protected with civil rights and would be given privileged victim status. Employee displays of offensive material would have to be allowed in the workplace. The case could even be made that since sexual orientation is an intrinsic characteristic and not a behavior, a company could not discipline employees for sexual acts committed in the workplace or during business trips. Laws that currently track convicted pedophiles might be found to be discriminatory, and serial child molesters might be able to live and work wherever they wanted, without anyone knowing about their past crimes. If you think that is far-fetched, just remember how far some judges have gone to put child murderers back on the streets or to allow mentally ill homeless people, who should be confined for their own protection, to terrorize neighborhoods.

The Back of the Bus

For more than thirty years, homosexual activists have sought to add sexual orientation to the 1964 Civil Rights Act, giving sodomy the same protection under the law as race.

Many black Americans are protesting the homosexual movement's usurpation of their civil rights struggle. African Americans came to this country as slaves. Under the Constitution slaves were counted as three-fifths of a person, which gave them no rights, but brought more power to their owners. For a century after the

Civil War, blacks were commonly denied the right to vote or allowed equal access to public facilities. That's real prejudice. No wonder blacks are angry when homosexuals claim to be victims of discrimination.

Defending his illegal sanctioning of same-sex marriages, San Francisco mayor Gavin Newsom said, "Rosa Parks didn't wait for the courts to tell her it was all right to ride in the front of the bus."

Many prominent black preachers were angered by that comment.

"We find the gay community's attempt to tie their pursuit of special rights based on their behavior to the civil rights movement of the 1960s and 1970s abhorrent. Being black is not a lifestyle choice." So said Bishop Andrew Merritt of Straight Gate International Church of Detroit, Michigan.

Even Rev. Jesse Jackson, founder and president of the Rainbow/PUSH Coalition, didn't like what Newsom had said.

"Gays were never called three-fifths human in the Constitution," Jackson told a group of Boston students. The point of civil rights legislation is to try to remedy social, political, and economic injustice. In America today, homosexuals are, per capita, one of the richest and most culturally and politically powerful groups in the nation.

Bishop Harry R. Jackson Jr. is chairman of the High Impact Leadership Coalition, a multiracial group of Christians who oppose ENDA, hate crimes laws, and other legislation aimed at undermining traditional family values. As Jackson says, he is "convinced that the black community is still in need of reviving and upgrading the civil rights movement. Like Bill Cosby, I believe that family restoration is at the heart of the problems that the black community faces. Yet there seems to be a growing attempt by the gay community to hijack the civil rights movement.

There has been an attempt to mask personal lifestyle preference as a civil rights issue. In addition, the radical gay movement seems to be seeking to silence the church."

A federal antidiscrimination law like ENDA would give the IRS even more power to investigate and rule against religious institutions. If a church was found to be discriminating against homosexuals by expressing Christian moral teaching, its tax-exempt status could be revoked. Given the political momentum of success following the passage of federal antidiscrimination legislation that included sexual orientation, homosexual activists would increasingly monitor the statements of religious leaders and attempt to insert themselves into religious organizations that dared to speak out against homosexual behavior. The hostility that many homosexuals now express toward the church and its moral teaching will become codified as law and will be supported by the preeminent power of the state.

For more than twenty years, radical homosexual activists have sought to undermine Christian moral teaching by threatening the tax-exempt status of churches that dared speak out against sodomy. In 1987, the National March on Washington for Lesbian and Gay Rights made this official demand: "Institutions that discriminate against lesbian and gay people should be denied tax-exempt status."

If ENDA is passed, then the common community conscience would be clear—antidiscrimination trumps freedom of speech. The door would be open for homosexual activists to begin censoring not just statements from the pulpit but also the Bible itself.

A new Colorado law passed in May 2008 and signed into law by Governor Bill Ritter is probably the most radical attempt yet to use the cover of "antidiscrimination" to censor Christians. The law made headlines because it made it illegal to deny a person access to public accommodations, including restrooms and locker rooms, based on sexual orientation as well as the perception of sexual orientation. Dr. James Dobson, the head of Focus on the Family, had this to say, "Henceforth, every woman and little girl will have to fear that a predator, bisexual, cross-dresser, or even a homosexual or heterosexual male might walk in and relieve himself in their presence."

Less well publicized are parts of the law that would make it a crime to publish "discriminative matter," i.e., publish works that appear to promote discrimination against sodomy. Read literally, the law makes it illegal to publish the Bible. Churches have an exemption, but other places of public accommodation, like bookstores and places of business, cannot sell or give away anything that is critical of homosexual activity, same-sex marriage, gay adoption, or any sexual orientation.

In Minneapolis, Minnesota, the homosexual group DignityUSA sued a Catholic meeting center for refusing to renew the group's lease due to theological disagreement. The church was found guilty of violating the city's civil rights ordinance based on "affectional preference." The church was liable for a $15,000 fine as well as legal costs. Luckily, the court of appeals overturned the ruling. But all that's needed is one victory in a case like that, and homosexuals will have taken a great step toward dictating the moral and theological teachings of individual churches.

With laws like ENDA on the books, they would be certain to win.

CHAPTER THIRTEEN

The Gospel of Hate

'Hate crimes' laws are a key part of a long-term strategy by homosexual activists to use 'sexual orientation'-based policies and laws to suppress dissent, radically redefine marriage, and, ultimately, to criminalize biblical morality.

–ROBERT H. KNIGHT, DIRECTOR OF
THE CULTURE AND FAMILY INSTITUTE

If hate crimes laws are passed, we're going to see the wholesale erosion of our freedoms as has never been seen in the history of this nation.

–JANET PARSHALL, FROM THE TV SERIES *SPEECHLESS*

When two employees of the city of Oakland, California, posted a flyer asking if any of their colleagues were interested in joining an informal group centered around the natural family, marriage, and family values, they never expected to be accused of hate speech.

Here is the text of the flyer in its entirety:

Preserve Our Workplace With Integrity

Good News Employee Association is a forum for people of faith to express their views on the contemporary issues of the day. With respect for the natural family, marriage, and family values.

If you would like to be a part of preserving integrity in the workplace, call Regina Rederford or Robin Christy.

Rederford and Christy are both Christians. They created the Good News Employee Association "in response to Bible bashing by ranking city officials and to the free rein given to radical left-wing groups over the city's e-mail and bulletin board systems." They were sick of the manner in which their office's Gay-Straight Employee Alliance was allowed to attack the Bible through widespread e-mails on the city's system. The alliance often derided Christian values as "antiquated" and referred to Christians as "hateful."

The day the Good News Employee Association flyer was posted, Joyce Hicks, the city's deputy director of the Community and Economic Development Agency, had it taken down. Shortly after, Hicks wrote a memo announcing a new antidiscrimination policy. In that memo, Hicks noted that some employees had been guilty of "inappropriately posting materials."

"Specifically," she wrote, "flyers were placed in public view that contained statements of a homophobic nature and were determined to promote sexual orientation-based harassment." Hicks warned that employees who posted such material could be fired.

Rederford and Christy sued Hicks and Oakland city manager Robert C. Bobb. The lawsuit argued that the policy of antidiscrimination as practiced was unconstitutional. As Scott Lively, Esq., of the Pro-Family Law Center argues, the announcement that Rederford and Christy had posted was "a completely affirmative and positive statement about a Christian value system centered on the natural family. For the city of Oakland to have interpreted that to mean an attack on homosexuality was really taking liberties."

U.S. District Court Judge Vaughn R. Walker ruled that Oakland had a right to prevent the Good News Employee Association from posting the flyer. The judge found that the city of Oakland's "legitimate administrative interests" outweighed the plaintiffs' rights to free speech. How can the terms "natural family," "marriage," and "family values" be considered disruptive to the efficient operation of the workplace? Because one lesbian employee objected to those words and labeled them "hate speech."

In his appeal on behalf of Rederford and Christy, Richard D. Ackerman of the Pro-Family Law Center argued that if Judge Walker's ruling were taken to its logical extreme, employees could be prohibited from announcing the birth of a child, or even from mentioning the fact that they were married, for fear of offending a co-worker. This argument is not far-fetched. As we have seen before, diversity counselors are already telling corporate America to avoid using words like "husband" and "wife." And some employees have been told that they can't have family photos in their workspaces for fear of offending their homosexual colleagues.

As bad as that sounds, however, there is something even more insidious in this case. Note that Deputy Director Hicks, the city of Oakland official who ordered the Good News announcement to be taken down, asserted that the poster had been "determined to promote sexual orientation-based harassment." Sexual harassment is against the law. It is usually dealt with as a civil matter, but it can also rise to the level of a crime. In effect, the new policy asserted that the group's announcement was promoting an illegal activity, possibly of a criminal nature.

This is a very serious matter. Laws equating the expression of Christian principles with promoting an illegal act put a terrible weapon in the hands of secularists who want to silence Christians. That's why we at the AFA have been working very hard to fight so-called "hate crimes" legislation. Hate crimes legislation can be made to sound like a good idea. But just as with antidiscrimination laws, hate crimes laws that include sexual orientation or gender identity will give liberal activists, judges, and prosecutors another tool to drive us from the public square.

Hate crimes laws increase penalties to include a criminal sentence when the defendant is convicted of having a "hateful intent" toward the victim based on the victim's membership in a protected group. First passed to protect African Americans and other minorities against racial violence, these laws are now being expanded to include sexual orientation as an identifying characteristic. That means adopting into law the principle that crimes committed against homosexuals should be punished more severely than crimes committed against other people, say, heterosexual Christians.

The Rhetoric of Motive

The usual argument for these laws is that they are necessary to stop gay bashing, a supposed epidemic of violence against homosexuals. If it were true that there was an epidemic of such violence, and if it were true that hate crimes laws would reduce such attacks, and if that were the primary effect and goal of hate crimes laws, then such laws might be justified. (Even then, if harsher punishments deter violent crimes, then why shouldn't we have harsher punishments for all assaults, regardless of the victim's sexual orientation?)

The problem is that there is little or no evidence for any of these assertions, especially the last one. Let me explain. In chapter seven ("The New Persecutors") we told the story of the "Philadelphia 11," the Christians who were arrested and jailed overnight for singing and preaching in a Philadelphia public park at a homosexual street festival. Five of them, including a seventeen-year-old girl, were bound over and charged with five felonies and three misdemeanors, meaning the defendants faced possible forty-seven-year prison sentences.

I think anyone would agree that felony charges, and a possible punishment of forty-seven years in prison is rather extreme, even if the Philadelphia 11 were guilty of *something*. I was not there, but suppose they were guilty of, oh, trespassing, or disturbing the peace. There is a long tradition of protest and civil disobedience in this country. It is not uncommon for protestors to violate the law in minor ways and to be appropriately punished if they do. But no one was hurt, no damage to property occurred, and when the police told the Philadelphia 11 to leave the event and head over to the place where they were to be arrested, they did so. And why the extraordinary aggression on the part of prosecutors?

Simple. Pennsylvania at the time had a hate crimes law on the books. (It has since been rescinded.) That law made a crime more serious if the motive was hostility toward people because of their sexual orientation. Both the letter and the spirit of the law made the Philadelphia 11 "more guilty" because they were Christians protesting against sodomy. Meanwhile, as we pointed out, homosexual protestors behaving in truly vile and even sacrilegious ways, not outside on public property but inside churches and private meeting places, are often not punished at all.

See what I mean about these laws being a new tool for the homosecularists? With hate crimes laws in their toolbox, their campaign to make Christian speech illegal becomes much easier. Of course, the secular liberals claim that they do not mean to do any such thing since hate crimes laws, in their view, aren't directed against speech. (In a way that's true, they're directed against thought!) But that's what homosecularists always claim—before they obtain whatever new power they want to use against us.

The most dangerous threat to Christians is a federal hate crimes law. There have been several attempts to get hate crimes laws passed through Congress. And though the wording differs, most such proposals would give the federal government the power to intervene in almost any criminal case normally prosecuted by a state if the U.S. Justice Department decided that the outcome (guilty or innocent) or the sentence was not sufficient to discourage crimes of bias or of bigotry. Normally, the federal government does not get involved in local crimes, like mugging or burglary or car theft or trespassing. The federal criminal code is almost all about white-collar crime, with some exceptions like kidnapping or certain bank robberies. But under a federal hate crimes law, the U.S. attorney general could decide to prosecute any such crimes if he decided that the defendants were motivated by either bias or bigotry.

The state's charges against the Philadelphia 11 were dropped after several months. Under a federal hate crimes statute, the federal government could have stepped in and charged them again. All the resources of the FBI and the U.S. Justice Department could have been brought to bear against those eleven Christians, including one seventeen-year-old girl.

OK, let's say that happens. The full investigative powers of the federal government have been unleashed. What will they look for? What will count as evidence?

Remember, under hate crimes laws it is not the crime, but the motive that matters. Now you might think, well, the police often look for motive. That's true in the sense that motive can help establish that someone suspected of a crime had a reason to commit it, giving the jury better reason to believe that the suspect is guilty. But that's not how motive is meant here. In the case of hate crimes law, the motive *is* the crime.

Let's say there is a special law against "greed crimes" that punishes criminals especially harshly for crimes motivated by greed. And let's say the police catch a bank robber red-handed, so there won't be any need to look for a motive as evidence in the usual sense. Under a greed-crime law, even though the police already know that the bank robber is guilty of bank robbery, they will begin looking for evidence that the suspect robbed the bank because he is greedy. They will proceed to interview people who know the robber, read his personal papers and diary, even look at the types of books and magazines he reads. If they find evidence proving that the robber is indeed a greedy person, he will then be guilty of a "greed crime" and will therefore be more harshly punished. The motive *is* the crime.

So to repeat, what would the FBI look for if it were to investigate the Philadelphia 11 under hate crimes laws? Simple. The agency would look at what the defendants read, whom they listen to or associate with—as in where they attend church—and what they talk about with their friends and neighbors. In other words, the FBI would look for evidence of how the defendants think. And mark my words, evidence that the Philadelphia 11 had the same beliefs that Christians who read the Bible and who support traditional Christian teachings about sex and marriage would surely be used as evidence that the "11" were also full of hatred for homosexuals.

After all, isn't that what the city of Oakland ruled when it forbade the Good News Employee Association from posting a flyer that never mentioned homosexuals but simply affirmed traditional family values? According to the city, that simple flyer was "determined to promote sexual orientation-based harassment." If affirming Christian values is harassment or hate speech, any evidence that someone holds such values can be used to prove someone guilty of a hate crime.

In 2005, a hate crimes bill passed the U.S. House of Representatives but failed in the Senate. That bill would have authorized federal intervention into any alleged crime under two conditions. The first condition was that the crime would have to be one that "interferes with commercial or other economic activity in which the victim is engaged at the time of the conduct" or "otherwise affects interstate or foreign commerce."

Translation: just about any crime at all would meet the first condition.

The second condition was "[t]he verdict or sentence obtained pursuant to state charges left demonstratively un-vindicated the federal interest in eradicating bias-motivated violence."

In other words, whenever a local jury or judge didn't hand out a conviction or a sentence that U.S. prosecutors thought would help discourage violence against a protected group, they could bring federal charges. That's just an invitation for homosexual advocates to pressure the federal government to help suppress their enemies. As Jan LaRue, chief counsel for Concerned Women for America commented at the time, "One can hardly imagine a more vague or broad invitation for federal prosecutors than 'un-vindicated' and 'federal interest.'" The law would give "the U.S. attorney general the discretion to enter any case he or she wants and will politicize criminal prosecution. Special interests will lobby to have their cases treated more seriously than other crime victims' and local authorities will be hapless to object."

In 2007, liberals in Congress tried, again unsuccessfully, to push through a hate crimes law. The bill was sponsored by Sen. Edward M. Kennedy who has called discrimination against homosexuality "an insidious aspect of American life." And he wants to make it into a crime.

For a long time, the ACLU opposed hate crimes legislation on the grounds that it would punish a belief, not an act. In 2007, the ACLU finally surrendered and endorsed Kennedy's bill, claiming that it would punish the act of discrimination, not the thought that motivated it. The only way to prove discrimination, however, would be to establish motive by examining expression or association.

The law in general and criminal law in particular is properly concerned with actions. When the law attempts to first identify and then punish certain thoughts, feelings, and beliefs, the law becomes a force for tyranny.

Under hate crimes laws, our personal expressions, the books we read, and the friends we have would all become potential evidence against us. The search for such evidence would allow law enforcement to investigate and to interpret forms of expression and association that had previously enjoyed protection under the First Amendment. Even if there is no prosecution, such investigations can have a "chilling effect" on free speech. The government does not have to jail or fine citizens to intimidate them from speaking their minds. Under state hate crimes laws and "human rights commissions," it's already happening.

Traverse City, Michigan, placed pro-homosexual rainbow stickers with the slogan "We are Traverse City" on all municipal vehicles. While the campaign was meant to counteract hate crimes, it only exacerbated tensions between traditional-minded citizens and the homosexual community. When David Leach, a thirty-year veteran of the Traverse City Police Department, organized local opposition to the stickers and made public comments against them, the city's human rights commission launched an investigation against him.

After the tragic murder of a young homosexual man, Matthew Shepard, homosexual activists publicly blamed Christian leaders like Dr. James Dobson for his death. This blurring of causality is the result of a moral confusion. First, the distinction between criticism and incitement to hatred is erased. Then, actual physical harm is inferred. As a result, any criticism is taken as a threat, and each threat is seen as violent.

In order to silence criticism of their own behavior, homosexual activists seek to make criticism against them a crime. Sometimes their rhetoric is more hateful than that which they seek to suppress. But Christians are supposed to be accepting because homosexuals' legal and social statuses as victims justify their hatred.

> The leaders of America's anti-gay industry are directly responsible for the continuing surge in hate violence against lesbian, gay, bisexual, and transgender people. . . . [C]hurch pews have been awash in ugly, anti-gay rhetoric, and fear-mongering.
>
> Matt Foreman, executive director,
> National Gay and Lesbian Task Force

Federal hate crimes proposals typically include monetary bonuses to local and state governments for prosecuting such crimes. Paying police departments and prosecutors to focus on certain crimes over others has huge potential for abuse. There is no persuasive evidence that crimes against homosexuals do not receive the same amount of attention and resources as other crimes. Any honest look at crime statistics would find that assaults by young African Americans against other young African Americans have the lowest clearance and conviction rates. If any group of crime victims has a claim to not receiving enough attention from the criminal justice officials, it is young African American men. Homosexuals take advantage of their elite status and support in the media to divert resources from America's real crime problem.

Federal hate crimes legislation would make homosexual activists' claims of an epidemic of gay bashing into a self-fulfilling prophecy. Whenever the federal government pays state and local governments to focus on a particular problem, that problem suddenly seems to become more prevalent. Statistics "follow the money." When the federal government began paying school systems huge bonuses for educating students with learning disabilities, schools began labeling kids "learning disabled" by the boatful. The same thing would happen with hate crimes.

One federal bill in consideration would establish federal grants of up to $100,000 for state and local officials both to investigate and prosecute hate crimes. This would create a powerful incentive for local law enforcement to find hate crimes, to categorize ordinary crimes as hate crimes, and to focus on these types of infractions rather than on others. When California enacted a similar law, hate crimes went up from a total of 75 to 2,052 in just four years.

Did Californians become that much more violent against homosexuals in such a short time? Of course not. The "surge" in hate crimes claimed by homosexual activists is clearly driven by programs that pay, or pressure, local governments to declare ordinary crimes hate crimes.

But what about all those high profile, headline-making incidents of gay bashing that we hear about? Well, they do happen. But, and I hesitate to say this because I don't want to give anyone an excuse to downplay real crimes against homosexuals or anyone else, it turns out that a shocking number of these headline cases are actually frauds. Concerned Women for America has compiled a partial list:

- At the University of Georgia, a homosexual resident-assistant reported that he had been victimized in nine hate crimes, including three supposed incidents of arson. When police questioned him, he admitted to committing the acts himself.
- A homosexual student at the College of New Jersey allegedly received death threats as did the homosexual student group in which he had served as treasurer. A large student rally was held, complete with faculty support, pro-gay T-shirts, and

buttons. Pink arm badges were handed out in "solidarity." Later the student admitted to police that he had sent the threats himself.

- A lesbian student at St. Cloud State University in Minnesota slashed her own face and falsely claimed that two men shouted anti-gay remarks at her and assaulted her. Students raised almost $12,000 as a reward for any information about her attackers.

- At Eastern New Mexico University, a lesbian student claimed that she had been attacked after her name was posted on an anti-gay "hit list" at a local laundromat. Police arrested her after a surveillance camera showed her posting the list.

- A lesbian in South Carolina was charged with giving false information to a police officer claiming that she had been beaten. Police said that she had hired a man to beat her so that she could report it as a hate crime.

- In Manchester, England, a homosexual minister faked a story about being raped. The staged attack prompted an intensive police investigation.

- In Mill Valley, California, a seventeen-year-old female wrestler at a local high school claimed that anti-gay epithets had been written on her car and on her school locker, and she had been pelted with eggs. The teenager, who was the leader of her school's gay-straight alliance, later admitted to authorities that she had perpetrated all of the incidents.

Advocates of hate crimes legislation like to focus on dramatic cases of violent crime. That's not surprising. As I say, if the point of hate crimes legislation really were to prevent murder and serious assault, I might be tempted to jump on the bandwagon.

What the hate crimes advocates don't tell you is that even under current law, many, perhaps even most, hate crimes don't involve violence. They involve speech. As Robert H. Knight, director of the Culture and Family Institute, pointed out during the 2005 debate on same-sex marriage held at Kent State University between himself and Elizabeth Birch, former executive director of the Human Rights Campaign, "More than half of the so-called 'hate crimes' in the last U.S. Justice Department report were categorized as 'intimidation' or 'simple assault,' which do not necessarily involve anything more than words. In terms of the proposed national hate crimes bill, this makes name-calling literally a federal case."

If groups like the ACLU would simply let the gears of justice turn without their political sabotage, then our society would have less crime, and people would feel more confident about the system.

Instead, we're heading down a road where our thoughts, motivations, and deeply held convictions may be turned against us. Under hate crimes statutes, Bibles, scriptural quotations, even book covers, and T-shirts that express religious beliefs have been labeled "hate speech." This means that an inspirational poster you have in your workspace or even a bumper sticker on your car can become a crime. Not only carrying a Bible into a public place but also printing and selling Bibles can be regarded as hate crimes.

The Web of Hate

The real threat of hate crimes laws can be understood only as part of an overall strategy, a "toolbox" as I call it, to silence Christians. A good carpenter or plumber does not carry just one tool; he has an entire toolbox. Some tools work in some situations and not in others. Some work together. Antidiscrimination laws create a legal and social environment conducive to the passage of hate crimes legislation because antidiscrimination laws effectively make criticism of the homosexual lifestyle an act of bigotry and thus illegal. Antibullying, diversity, and sex-education curricula prepare future generations to accept homosexuality as normal and to question their parents' moral authority. The Fairness Doctrine, or similar controls over broadcasting content, would restrict the debate over these important issues. And the threat to the tax-exempt status of religious organizations silences potential opponents.

Hate crimes legislation is another tool for homosecularists to use where others have failed. Rev. Rob Schenck, a pro-life minister, was sitting in the courtroom during the U.S. Supreme Court arguments in the *Dale v. Boy Scouts of America* case. Seated next to Schenck was the Clinton White House liaison for gay and lesbian issues. The official must have thought that Schenck was a fellow liberal because she whispered to him, "We're not going to win this case, but that's OK. Once we get 'hate crimes' laws on the books, we're going to go after the Scouts and all the other bigots."

As Christians, we understand that the First Amendment protects speech that we find offensive and even blasphemous. We accept that. After all, it was because Christians, and Christian pastors especially, demanded constitutional protection for freedom of religion that we have a First Amendment in the first place. But having insisted on inserting the First Amendment in the Constitution to protect all Americans, we certainly insist on its protections for ourselves. The government does not have the right to bind our consciences or prohibit us from expressing our beliefs. The government has no right to decide nor even influence the doctrine of any church or of any citizen.

Christians do not seek official victim status. Acts of persecution against Christians can be remedied under existing laws. There are already laws against vandalism, assault, and harassment.

At the same time, we must be realistic about the threat we face. Hate crimes laws have very little to do with hate or with crime. The primary goal of these laws is to silence Christians who object morally to sodomy and who object politically to the attempt of the secularist elite to dominate our culture and to subject our children to their own beliefs and to their own desires. We have no intention to be silenced.

CHAPTER FOURTEEN

O, Canada!

The future is clearly the Canadian way.

—EVAN WOLFSON, AMERICAN HOMOSEXUAL ACTIVIST
AND DIRECTOR OF FREEDOM TO MARRY

The problems caused by hate crimes laws facing people in Canada are just a taste of what we can expect here, if we don't put a stop to efforts to silence us.

—JANET PARSHALL, FROM THE TV SERIES *SPEECHLESS*

As a youth pastor in Canada, Stephen Boissoin worked with kids from all walks of life. He was a father figure to them, the cool kids and the loners, the straight kids and those struggling with sexual identity. He ministered to them all. But when he felt that the homosexual machine was pushing its agenda to the detriment of children, he put his feelings into words and sent a letter to the editor of his local paper, the *Red Deer Advocate*. The fallout from that simple act is a chilling example of what could happen if America were to follow Canada's example by passing its own hate crimes laws and antidiscrimination laws.†

Ending up on the same path as Canada's might not even require an act of Congress. Liberals are already successfully pushing the idea that the U.S. Supreme Court should take the laws of other nations into account when interpreting our Constitution. The U.S. Supreme Court has already given in to that idea in two important cases, both of which benefit homosexual activists. And state supreme courts have done the same. What was done to

Stephen Boissoin and other Canadians and to subjects of the United Kingdom and other European nations could happen here.

Through his ministry, Boissoin was beginning to see how teenagers were being manipulated into believing that homosexuality was "normal, necessary, acceptable, and productive." (This is the exact wording of a government-funded program used in the public schools.) Boissoin learned that a public school teacher who had founded a pro-homosexual group in a local high school was inviting an openly homosexual minister to teach youth a homosexual version of the Bible. Boissoin says, "I absolutely believe in tolerance. . . . If that's the way they want to live their lives [practicing a homosexual lifestyle], they should have that right to do so." But he adds, "Where the boundaries were overstepped was when my tax dollars—and it's not about money—were used to fund an initiative that was absolutely against my values as a human being and a Christian."

Boissoin wrote a letter to the editor that was meant to be hard-hitting, yet understanding of those tempted by homosexuality. His letter begins:

> The following is not intended for those who are suffering from an unwanted sexual identity crisis. For you I have understanding, care, compassion, and tolerance. I sympathize with you and offer you my love and fellowship.†

The letter goes on to describe the efforts of homosexual activists:

> Your children are being warped into believing that same-sex families are acceptable, that men kissing men is appropriate. . . . The homosexual agenda is not gaining ground

because it is morally backed. It is gaining ground because you, Mr. and Mrs. Heterosexual, do nothing to stop it.†

The fallout from the publication of the letter was swift and severe. Because Canada has hate crimes laws on the books, Stephen Boissoin found himself facing criminal charges.†

For writing a letter.

Citizens of Canada do not enjoy the same First Amendment protections of free speech that we do in America. In late April 2004, the Canadian Parliament amended the criminal code to add sexual orientation to the list of subjects upon which Canadians may not speak in a hateful way. Citizens found to be speaking in a hateful way are subject to prosecution by the attorney general. Which is what happened to Stephen Boissoin.

Red Deer teacher Darren Lund filed a complaint with the Alberta Human Rights and Citizenship Commission.† Part of the complaint alleged that as a direct result of Boissoin's letter a teenager was assaulted on the basis of sexual orientation. In other words, Boissoin's letter was not just viewed as hate speech but as an incitement to violence that provoked at least one assault.

Five years and tens of thousands of Canadian dollars in legal fees later, Stephen Boissoin was found guilty of discrimination by the Alberta Human Rights and Citizenship Commission. Boissoin was prohibited from making "disparaging remarks" about homosexuals in the future and was ordered to remove any such expressions from the Web site of his organization, the Concerned Christian Coalition. He was ordered to pay $5,000 (Canadian) to the plaintiff for damages as well as expenses for a witness who appeared at the human rights panel to testify against him.†

Recalling his years of legal struggles, Boissoin says he was initially angry not only with his persecutors but also with God. But as time passed, one thing he learned in the process was a renewal of his faith. "Just depend on Him," says Boissoin, "and say as a Christian, 'God, regardless, whether I'm found guilty, regardless of whether people like me, I'm going to hold true to Your Word. I am going to continue to hold true to Your Word and stand strong.' And that's what I'm going to do."

The problems caused by hate crimes laws in Canada are a warning to us in America. The goal of these laws is to silence Christians. These laws will make it a criminal act to speak in opposition to homosexuality in public venues.

Bullying the Pulpit

Don't believe anyone who tells you that this won't have an effect on what pastors can say in their own pulpits. Even if U.S. hate crimes laws specifically exempt clergymen from preaching in church, the very fact that Christian principles are defined as hate speech when uttered outside of churches will just add one more brick to the wall the secularists are building to keep Christians out of public life. If Christian speech is legally defined as bigotry, but pastors are allowed to get away with it "on a technicality," how long do you think even pastors will be able to hold out? How long before the IRS shows up? How long before some ambitious prosecutor decides that a homosexual mugging is really the fault of Pastor Smith who preaches the biblical view of sodomy? The principle we must understand is that the law changes our culture, and then our culture changes the law. If the law teaches that Christian truth is bigotry in a discussion around the water cooler or a in a letter to the editor, our culture absorbs the message until the "special exemption" for pastors will seem irrational. Isn't a bigot a bigot? Why should we tolerate bigots anywhere?

Cases in Europe have already brought these laws into the church sanctuary. Expression of Christian beliefs, biblical texts such as the Ten Commandments, and even the words "natural family," "marriage," and "family values" have been legally charged as hate speech.

Hate crimes laws are a slippery slope—one that Canada is already well on its way down. Tristan Emmanuel is the former president of Equipping Christians for the Public Square Centre and author of *Christophobia: The Real Reason Behind Hate Crime Legislation*. He has some idea of what a United States under hate crimes laws might look like.†

Emmanuel notes that since the 1960s, churches in Canada have been silent about human sexuality. And it's only gotten worse with hate crimes laws on the books:

> Most pastors don't want to spend time in the courts. They don't want to be criminalized for basically sharing the love of Jesus Christ. And so we completely shy away from that legitimate avenue of discussion—morality, because it's now become politicized.
>
> Tristan Emmanuel, from the TV series
> *Speechless*, episode three

I am not saying that hate crimes laws will result in lots of arrests and jail time. That would be unpopular and there would be no need for it. Jail is what we use to deter real criminals because there is little else society can take away from those who break the law other than their freedom. Law-abiding citizens can be intimidated by loss of reputation, legal expenses, a call from the IRS, even a letter from the ACLU. Most of the time, law-abiding Christians are intimidated by their own lawyers, who, knowing the political and legal risks, are constantly urging employers including churches to "overcomply" with the law and to censor their actions to avoid even the most modest legal risks.†

By allowing liberals and homosexual activists to impose their politically correct constraints, Christians end up muzzling certain aspects of the Gospel when the Gospel should be taught as a comprehensive whole. Today, according to Emmanuel, Christians in Canada are prepared to share the non-controversial aspects of the Gospel with everyone. But Canadian Christians purposely shy away from the moral teaching of sexuality.

> The Gospel doesn't make sense if you don't establish the context for the Gospel, i.e., sin and repentance. People do things that need to be repented of. And though it may be politically incorrect to say that, it needs to be said. Otherwise, the antidote, which is Jesus, doesn't make sense.
>
> Tristan Emmanuel, from the TV
> series *Speechless*, episode three

Many Americans are following the Canadian and European models of approaching the Gospel like a buffet, selecting the teachings they like and avoiding those they don't. This selective reading of the Gospel is particularly popular with Democratic politicians who want to appeal to their left-wing base without alienating Christian voters. Barack Obama gave us a perfect example of this when he proclaimed that he was not "willing to accept a reading of the Bible that considers an obscure line in Romans to be more defining of Christianity than the Sermon on the Mount."

President Obama is of course free to interpret the Gospel as he chooses. But his belittling of biblical restraints against homosexuality is based on a selective reading. Jesus didn't teach us to follow the Ten Commandments according to our lifestyle choices. The Gospel is a complete and universal moral vision. When we ignore its teachings as being "obsolete" or even unjust, we are allowing temporal worldliness to triumph over eternal faith.

Hate crimes laws make it illegal to teach the Gospel the way it is supposed to be, in its entirety. In Canada, when alleged hate speech is investigated and prosecuted by tribunals such as the Alberta Human Rights and Citizenship Commission, the result is not equal rights under the law but persecution of politically disfavored individuals.

This is possible only in a nation that has lost its moral bearings. Political correctness replaces traditional morality with sensitivity, but sensitivity only to the feelings of a few privileged individuals whose feelings are so tender that they require legal protection.

- When William G. Whatcott, a Saskatchewan resident and former homosexual, distributed flyers listing the medical dangers of homosexual behavior, he was charged with hate speech. In ruling against Whatcott, Anil K. Pandila, chairman of the Saskatchewan Human Rights Tribunal, said that it didn't matter whether the information in the material Whatcott distributed was true. Whatcott had to pay $17,500 in damages to four homosexual plaintiffs, who claimed to have been injured by what Whatcott said in the flyers.

- The same tribunal ordered the *Saskatoon StarPhoenix* newspaper to pay three gay men $1,500 each after the newspaper agreed to run a paid advertisement that featured Bible verses critical of homosexual behavior. The individual who created and bought space for the ad was also fined.

- The Alberta Human Rights and Citizenship Commission investigated a Catholic bishop in Calgary for comments he made about homosexuality and same-sex marriage in his pastoral letter to parishioners and in a column he wrote for the *Calgary Sun* newspaper.

And it's not just happening in Canada:

- An Anglican bishop in Great Britain was fined for refusing to hire an openly gay applicant for the position of diocesan youth officer.
- A British couple in Fleetwood, Lancashire, was questioned by police on possible hate crimes charges after they wrote a letter to their local city council criticizing officials for distributing magazines in its office promoting homosexual behavior and for taking pro-gay stances.
- Catholic bishops in Belgium and Spain were sued for violating antidiscrimination laws for making public statements in opposition to homosexual behavior and same-sex marriage.
- A British couple that had fostered twenty-eight young children in just six years was forced to give one of the children up after refusing to comply with legislation requiring them to treat homosexuality as morally equivalent to heterosexuality.

Imposing "International Law" on America

Our First Amendment does help protect freedoms of religious belief, expression, and assembly. Because Canada does not have anything like a First Amendment, it has been much easier for homosexual activists to use hate crimes laws against Christians. For the same reason, the Canadian government can censor speech or religious expression.

Both Dr. Laura Schlesinger and Dr. James Dobson, syndicated radio talk show hosts, have been warned by Canadian broadcasting regulators that their broadcasts will be edited for hate speech whenever they discuss homosexuality. In their formal rebuke of Schlesinger's remarks on homosexuality, the Canadian Broadcast Standards Council made very clear that the First Amendment stops at the border: "In Canada, we respect freedom of speech, but we don't worship it."

Now our First Amendment protections are endangered by a growing movement toward adopting international law as an arbiter of U.S. constitutional rights. No one is ever going to get the First Amendment repealed. Yet precisely because other countries don't have anything like the First Amendment, judges can weaken our Constitution by importing foreign legal principles.

Both the 2003 *Lawrence v. Texas* U.S. Supreme Court decision legalizing sodomy throughout the United States and the 2003 *Goodridge v. Department of Public Health* case by the Massachusetts Supreme Judicial Court legalizing same-sex marriage in that state cited international law as precedent. The Massachusetts judges referred to a Canadian same-sex marriage decision in their opinion. Writing for the majority in *Lawrence*, Supreme Court Justice Anthony M. Kennedy cited the European Court of Human Rights as precedent. After that decision, Justice Stephen Breyer said, "[How] our Constitution . . . fits into the governing documents of other nations I think will be a challenge for the next generation."

In other words, if the Constitution does not allow certain aspects of the liberal or secularist or homosexual agendas, then American judges should use the laws of other nations as a tool to force the secularist agenda on us.

It is clear that we can no longer count on the Constitution alone to protect fundamental freedoms in the United States.

> 2003 ACLU International
> Civil Liberties Report

Why have the ACLU and its allies turned from the most ingenious form of government ever designed by man to international law? Probably because they know that even with their broad theories and legal demands, the U.S. Constitution can be stretched only so far, so fast to advance their radical agenda.

Alan Sears and Craig Osten,
The Homosexual Agenda: Exposing the
Principal Threat to Religious Freedom Today

One reason liberals love this idea is that if American courts are allowed to adjust our laws to conform to those of other nations, that means judges get to pick which countries' laws should guide the United States. Do they mean European laws or Islamic sharia law? Perhaps we should use Islamic divorce law but European law for same-sex marriage? Liberals would love that.

Same-sex marriages have been legal in Holland and in Belgium since 2003 and in Spain and Canada since 2005. Denmark, Germany, France, and Great Britain all recognize same-sex "partnerships," giving them most of the rights of married couples, without the legal recognition of marriage. The French government has made "homophobia" a crime punishable by a year in prison and a fine of EUR 45000. Great Britain recently lowered the age of consent for homosexual acts to sixteen. Prostitution is legal in Holland.

Meanwhile, homosexual acts are punishable by prison sentences in many countries.

There is no international consensus on law. And "international law" in the sense that liberals mean it is a fiction. Aside from treaties and trade agreements, temporary, contingent, and mostly unenforceable, international law does not exist. What liberal jurists and activists really mean when they appeal to international law is international opinion, by which they mean elite *opinion* in other select, no-longer-Christian nations, namely Western Europe and Canada.

Traditional family values aren't important to us anymore. They are something we do research on, like a fossil.

Ebba Witt–Brattström, professor
of comparative literature and feminist
commentator, Stockholm University

When liberals say America needs to follow international law, they usually mean that they value the opinion of the decadent, anti-Christian global elite over the binding law of the U.S. Constitution.

Judge Robert H. Bork said it this way, "International law is not law but politics. For that reason, it is dangerous to give the name 'law,' which summons up respect, to political struggles that are essentially lawless. [The result is that] international law becomes one more weapon in the domestic culture war."

Homosexual activists are using appeals to international law to advance an agenda that is unconstitutional, anti-democratic, and abhorrent to a majority of Americans. Like the Muslims, homosexuals are creating their own international community, respecting no borders and identifying primarily with their own individual "tribe," which is scattered throughout the world. When homosexuals appeal to international law and international standards of morality and culture, they always do so with an eye toward the society that is the most lax in its morals.

If that doesn't sound like the world you want to live in, you have to take a stand and make your voice heard.

Janet Parshall, from the TV series *Speechless*

A group affiliated with the United Nations Commission on Human Rights (UNCHR) tried to add sexual orientation to the commission's antidiscrimination code. Two former ACLU members were part of the group. During a meeting, homosexual activists called for a "showdown with religion." The effort failed, but it demonstrates the degree to which homosecularists wish to impose immoral norms on America from outside its borders. Clearly, the UNCHR proposal was not meant seriously to change anti-homosexual policies of Muslim countries.

The nation that is closest to the United States, both physically and culturally, is Canada. Changes in Canadian law can have direct effects on the American legal and political system. Lambda Legal Defense and Education Fund already provides detailed information on how American homosexuals can be married in Canada and then return and petition in the United States for recognition of their marriage by their employers and state governments.

Laws like the Canadian hate crimes laws are the logical consequence of the propaganda campaign we are already experiencing in our own public schools, the one that defines safe schools as places where homosexuals are protected from hate speech, and hate speech is defined as any criticism at all. They are the logical consequence of defining Christian belief as bigotry. They are the logical consequence of turning ordinary citizens or employees into pariahs for defending Christian principles. In short, they are the logical consequence of exactly what is happening in the United States today.

CHAPTER FIFTEEN

The Last Battle

We have captured the liberal establishment and the press. We have already beaten you on a number of battlefields. And we have the spirit of the age on our side. You have neither the faith nor the strength to fight us, so you might as well surrender now. . . . We are going to force you to recant everything you have believed or have said about sexuality. . . . Finally we will in all likelihood want to expunge a number of passages from your scriptures and rewrite others, eliminating preferential treatment of marriage and using words that will allow for homosexual interpretations of passages.

—MICHAEL SWIFT, "WARNING TO THE HOMOPHOBES,"
GAY COMMUNITY NEWS

The battle for marriage will be the decisive conflict in a new war on Christianity. If we lose this battle, the Christian faith itself will be designated by our own government as a form of bigotry. Christians and Christian ideas will be stigmatized, repressed, and forced out of the public sphere.

This is not my prediction. It is, at least for some major activists, their openly stated goal.

And it is the inescapable and logical conclusion of putting same-sex unions on the same legal, moral, and cultural footing as married love.

The law is a teacher. It is simply not possible in a democratic society to tolerate any group, such as Christians, that resists a moral teaching, once that moral teaching is raised to the force of law. Same-sex marriage teaches society that a same-sex union is morally indistinguishable from marriage between a man and a woman. After same-sex marriage becomes law, anyone who believes there is something special or different about the union of a husband and a wife will be regarded both legally and morally as engaging in irrational and hateful bigotry.

The cultural and legal pressures unleashed by this governmental declaration of moral equivalence will be extremely powerful. In some cases, same-sex marriage will force Christians and other believers to choose between following their consciences and obeying the law. In effect, the elevation of same-sex marriage to a constitutional right will result in devaluation of, government-enforced exclusion of, and even persecution of Christian moral teaching.

The process by which same-sex marriage started to become legal was calculatedly undemocratic, as it had to be. Most Americans do not support redefining the basic meaning of marriage to fit same-sex relationships. As I write, the latest poll shows that only 30 percent of Americans favor same-sex marriage.

The federal Defense of Marriage Act (DOMA), overwhelmingly passed in 1996 by both Democrats and Republicans, affirms marriage for federal purposes as the legal union between one man and one woman and provides that states are not required to recognize same-sex marriages of another state. Twenty-one states have DOMA in effect. Currently, thirty states have passed state constitutional marriage amendments banning same-sex marriages, including Florida, Arizona, and California, which voted on marriage amendments on November 4, 2008. Forty-one states prohibit same-sex nuptials, either by statute or by amendment.

But these laws are subject to change. Gay-marriage advocates are succeeding with stealth campaigns to change the laws through the judiciary in a few select states, knowing that one state could open the floodgates for many others. Currently, both Connecticut and Massachusetts allow same-sex marriages.

California's highest court recently agreed to hear several legal challenges to California's newest state ban on same-sex marriage. The California Supreme Court accepted three lawsuits that seek to nullify Proposition 8, a constitutional amendment approved by voters in November 2008. Proposition 8 had in turn overruled the court's decision of May 2008 to legalize gay marriage. The battle in California to ban gay marriage was won by voters in November 2008, but for how long?

The ACLU has played a major role in actively trying to prevent voters from having the right to vote for traditional marriage by keeping initiatives off the ballot and challenging them in court once voters pass them.

After Alaska overwhelmingly passed a constitutional amendment protecting traditional marriage, former ACLU executive director Ira Glasser said, "Today's results prove that certain fundamental issues should not be left up to a majority vote."

In other words, when the people have spoken, the ACLU doesn't feel obliged to listen if they don't like what they hear. If America is not "ready" for the gay-marriage agenda, then it's up to them to prepare us. What they were unable to achieve democratically, they will try to win by judicial fiat.

On November 18, 2003, the Massachusetts Supreme Judicial Court declared that its government must accept same-sex unions as marriages. Six months later, the first gay couples were getting "married" in that state.

While activists sought the courts' help to force their moral views upon the general public, whenever the people spoke, same-sex marriage was repudiated, even in supposedly progressive states like Wisconsin, Oregon, and Michigan. In fact, even in California. In 2000, California voters approved a referendum defining marriage as one man and one woman—by a margin of more than 60 percent.

Despite this overwhelming majority vote of the people, on May 15, 2008, the California Supreme Court ruled that this referendum, passed directly by the people, was unconstitutional. With this decision, the court unilaterally imposed same-sex marriage on the entire state. As San Francisco Mayor Gavin Newsom so memorably put it, gay marriage was on its way "whether you like it or not."

The court declared its same-sex decision would not "diminish any other person's constitutional rights" or "impinge upon the religious freedom of any religious organization, official, or any other person." But that is just what same-sex marriage will do, must do, and is doing already.

What did the California court say? It said that orientation is a protected class just like race. California's highest court ruled that people who see any difference at all between two men pledging permanent sodomy and a husband and wife are the same as bigots who oppose interracial marriage.

Put that legal principle into the law, that is, "There is no difference between same-sex couples and opposite-sex couples, and anyone who disagrees is just bigoted," and there will be very large legal and cultural consequences for the many Americans like you and me who disagree. "Equality" arguments elevated into constitutional principles by powerful judges don't lead to live-and-let-live tolerance. They lead to expansion of the power of government to repress "anti-equality" ideas, institutions, and people. And once gay marriage becomes law, anyone who opposes it will be viewed in legal terms as "anti-equality," which is what is happening right now in California to the Mormons, Rick Warren's Saddleback Church, and other religious groups who supported Proposition 8.

The fastest way to see what lies ahead for Christians (as well as for any other traditional-faith community) is to ask: How does the law and government treat bigots who oppose interracial marriage? In 1967, the U.S. Supreme Court ruled that state governments could not ban interracial marriages. Once this principle was put into law it took less than twenty years and no further government action—that is, no further law passed by Congress, no further action by any elected official accountable to voters—for the Internal Revenue Service to decide to strip a fundamentalist Christian university (Bob Jones University) of its federal tax-exempt status because the school forbade interracial marriage and dating.

I hope I don't have to add that I personally see no comparison between same-sex unions and interracial marriage. Racism is morally wrong, and bans on interracial marriage have no deep or enduring roots in Christian thought. My sole goal is to point out what it means legally, morally, and culturally for Christians when courts, urged on by liberal secularists, act on the idea that those of us who oppose treating same-sex unions as marriages are just like racists who oppose interracial marriage.

Maggie Gallagher, president of the National Organization for Marriage (www.nationformarriage.org), explains the real difference between the same-sex issue and the interracial-marriage issue: "Bans on interracial marriage were about keeping two races separate so that one race could oppress the others, and that was bad. Marriage is about bringing together the two great halves of humanity, male and female, in part so that children can know and be known by, love and be loved by, their own mom and dad. And that's good."

Here's my point. Legal principles are powerful things. The legal principle that leads to gay marriage is this: There is no good reason why anyone would want to define marriage as the union of a husband and a wife. Only irrational malice and hatred explains why marriage means a man and a woman.

The necessary cultural and legal corollary is that people and organizations that refuse to treat same-sex couples exactly the same as husbands and wives are evil discriminators who must be marginalized, repressed, and, where possible, punished.

Even civil unions can have the same legal effect if they are predicated on courts adopting the basic moral and legal principle of "no difference" equality between same-sex and opposite-sex unions.

Case in point. On October 25, 2006, the New Jersey Supreme Court ordered the legislature to create either same-sex marriage or civil unions on the grounds that the state's marriage laws were discriminatory in intent because they excluded same-sex couples.

How long did it take for a Christian group to face punishment by the government for its refusal to treat same-sex unions equivalent to marriages? Not twenty years, but less than one year.

No More Weddings

Ocean Grove, New Jersey, is a town right out of a Victorian novel. It was here, in 1873, that Fanny Crosby wrote the beloved hymn, "Blessed Assurance." Only one square mile in area, Ocean Grove looks like "the town time forgot," and there's a good reason for it. Back in 1870, the state of New Jersey granted a charter to the Ocean Grove Camp Meeting Association, whose trustees are all members of the United Methodist Church. The town was established with the purpose of making it "a perpetual oblation upon Christ's altar, enjoining its strict observance upon those who may succeed us."†

The Camp Meeting Association owns all of the land in Ocean Grove, as well as the boardwalk, beach, and water rights.

The boardwalk in Ocean Grove is not like others on the Jersey shore. There are no tattoo parlors or gambling establishments. The only structure on the boardwalk is a church pavilion used for religious services. The pavilion is at the center of a controversy that threatens the sanctity of every house of worship in America.†

The pavilion is an open-air structure that looks out onto the ocean. Sunday worship services attract as many as six hundred people in the summer. Daily Bible classes are also offered. The pavilion is open to the public, whether they want to worship or just relax in the shade.

> Our mission here on the boardwalk is that people who would just be happening by would hear the Gospel, would hear the music, would hear the praise, would be drawn in. And one of the things that we notice every single week, from our first worship service at the beginning of the summer to our last, is every week, there's a conversion for Jesus Christ. Every single week. A lot of times it's people who didn't intend to go to church that day. And that's what makes this particular facility for us so vitally important, because it's exactly what our mission is about.
>
> Scott Hoffman, chief administrative officer,
> Ocean Grove Camp Meeting Association,
> from the TV series *Speechless*, episode five

For years, Ocean Grove has hosted weddings in the pavilion. You don't have to be a Methodist. Anyone who wants to can rent the facility. When a lesbian couple, Harriet Bernstein and Luisa Paster, asked to have their civil-union ceremony performed in the pavilion, Ocean Grove refused because hosting same-sex ceremonies on church property violated Methodist church law.

Did Harriet and Luisa, exercising their freedom to enter a

civil union, simply find another site for their ceremony? Of course not. This is America. They reached for their lawyer and a way to punish the folks who dared to disagree with them. And why not? In their view, now endorsed by the New Jersey Supreme Court, the Ocean Grove Methodists are evil discriminators who need to be punished.

The couple filed complaints (along with another same-sex couple similarly refused) with the New Jersey attorney general's office in the Division of Civil Rights. Their charge? Orientation discrimination. Before the Supreme Court decision ordering same-sex unions to be treated just like marriages, there would have been no grounds for such a complaint. Marriages had a special legal status, and a group didn't have to allow any other kind of ceremony because it held weddings.

But a few months later a bureaucrat in the New Jersey Department of Environmental Protection ruled that Ocean Grove should be stripped of its state real estate tax exemption on the beach pavilion solely because the Methodist group was discriminating against same-sex couples. This ruling followed a request by Garden State Equality, the gay-marriage advocacy group in New Jersey, to revoke Ocean Grove's tax exemption as a religious organization.

Scott Hoffman saw the writing on the wall. If Ocean Grove did fight back, they might be distracted from their mission by long and costly civil rights proceedings.

Ocean Grove asked the federal court for an injunction to keep the state from infringing on its rights, based on First Amendment guarantees of free exercise of religion and free association, but was turned down. The federal judge ruled that it would be improper for a federal court to stop the state's Division of Civil Rights from investigating the lesbian couples' complaints since the state has an important interest in preventing discrimination in a place of public accommodation.

Ocean Grove has the right to use their property consistent with their religious faith.

> Brian Raum, Alliance Defense Fund

Weddings are only a small part of Ocean Grove's mission. There is a gospel music ministry series, a camp meeting series, and a youth program held every morning called "Breakfast Club." Ocean Grove also performs outreach programs and partners together with charitable organizations and the local chamber of commerce in town. But according to the gay-marriage advocacy group at Garden State Equality, this wonderful ministry can and should be punished by the government by losing its tax-exempt status for following biblical doctrine.

Can a Christian group really be deprived of its tax exemption because it won't treat same-sex unions the same as marriages? It's already happened—in Ocean Grove, New Jersey.

This is one small sign of what's to come. Under the public accommodations law, a great many professions may become closed to Christians who cannot, in good conscience, assist in or celebrate a permanent pledge of sodomy as if it were a marriage.

Small business owners may find that they have to offer the same marriage discounts to homosexual couples as they also offer to heterosexual couples. Teachers who refer to marriage as being between a woman and a man would face administrative discipline. That's already happened in Boston where public school teachers have been threatened with termination if they failed to portray same-sex marriage in a positive light. A Christian wedding photographer in New Mexico has actually been fined by the state government for turning down the chance to photograph a same-sex couple's commitment ceremony.

This is exactly what the homosecularists have wanted all along. The architects of same-sex marriage want to use the law to reshape the culture so that disagreement with their views on homosexual relations becomes the moral, cultural, and *legal* equivalent of racism.

The religious freedom threats from same-sex marriage are not an accidental byproduct; for too many liberal secularist leaders, they are the point. Under civil rights laws any business that caters to the general public is a "public accommodation." And no public accommodation can refuse service to a protected minority.

> If you are a public accommodation and you are open to anyone on Main Street that means you must be open to everyone on Main Street. If they don't do it, that's contempt and they will go to jail.
>
> Sean Kososky, the Triangle Foundation

No More Charity

In 1903, Boston's Catholic Charities began placing orphaned Catholic children in Catholic homes. The services provided by the organization proved so valuable that Catholic Charities widened its scope to provide adoption services for families and children of all faiths. Eventually it became one of the largest adoption agencies in the state. Working closely with state agencies, Catholic Charities placed scores of children in foster and adoptive homes every year. The organization made a specialty of handling "special needs" children who have a harder time being adopted and who need specially trained and dedicated staff. In recent years, some 80 percent of the cases handled by Catholic Charities involved children with special needs. The Massachusetts Department of Social Services provided Catholic Charities with about $1 million annually (out of Catholic Charities' total budget of $38 million) to help with special needs cases.

In November 2003, the Massachusetts Supreme Judicial

Court established same-sex marriage. Catholic Charities realized that it would now face legally married same-sex couples requesting placements. The charity would either have to violate Catholic views publicly by treating these couples the same as other married couples or break the law.

This was not simply an issue of equal access to state funding. It's illegal to run an adoption agency without a license in Massachusetts, and the government would no longer give a religious adoption agency a license after same-sex marriage became law unless the agency solemnly pledged to treat same-sex couples exactly the same as a husband and wife.

Catholic Charities of Boston asked for a very narrow legal exemption and even agreed to refer same-sex couples who wished to adopt to any one of the other eighty adoption agencies that were willing to do same-sex couple adoptions. Let me emphasize that it was not a debate about whether gay couples could adopt. They already had that legal right. It was a public and legal debate about whether the government was going to permit a single adoption agency to act according to Christian moral rules.

The answer was a resounding, "No." It is shocking but very telling about what lies ahead, to hear how powerful politicians in Massachusetts described the Catholic Church and its simple desire to keep assisting helpless children in finding homes without violating the tenets of the Christian faith. Massachusetts politicians, both Democrats and Republicans, reasoned: "We wouldn't grant an exemption to an adoption agency that discriminated against interracial couples, so why should we let Catholic Charities stay in the adoption business if it 'discriminates' against same-sex couples?"

"It is reprehensible that any governor would support a policy of discrimination against any group of people, regardless of whether the discrimination is based on race or creed or sexual preference," said Philip W. Johnston, chairman of the state Democratic Party in

Massachusetts. Rep. Salvatore F. DiMasi, speaker of the House, said that the state must "ensure that discrimination is not tolerated in this vital publicly supported function." The *Boston Globe* opined: "Catholic Charities must not discriminate."

Even the Republican candidate for governor Kerry Healey joined the chorus, "I believe that any institution that wants to provide services that are regulated by the state has to abide by the laws of this state, and our antidiscrimination laws are some of the most important."

Of course homosecularist leaders went even further, "What these bishops are doing is shameful, wrong, and has nothing to do whatsoever with faith," Joe Solmonese, president of the Human Rights Campaign, pronounced of the Catholics' desire not to be forced to place children with same-sex couples.

This is what inevitably happens when a falsehood—there is no difference between same-sex union and marriage—is elevated to a moral principle and inserted into the law, to be used as a tool by activist judges.

After one hundred years of services, Catholic Charities adoption services was forced to close its doors. Prof. John H. Garvey, dean of the Boston College Law School, wrote an article in the *Boston Globe* on March 14, 2006, with a very telling title: "State putting Church out of adoption business." That's nondiscrimination for you.

If same-sex marriage is made legal in other states, and supported by antidiscrimination laws that elevate sexual orientation to a protected status, many other Christian social ministries will be forced to make similar choices.

In Canada, an evangelical ministry that provides group homes to disabled adults was recently ordered by the government to develop a re-education plan after it tried to insist its employees believe and act upon Christian sexual teachings.

No More Democracy

Citizens who sign petitions to protect marriage, or who have donated to this cause, have found themselves to be victims of harassment, intimidation, and even political retribution.

Leo "Skip" Childs is the chief of the rescue squad in North Truro, a small town on Cape Cod, Massachusetts. When his church circulated a petition for a statewide referendum on a measure to define marriage as the union of one man and one woman, Childs signed it. Childs was up for reappointment to the board of fire engineers in his town. A selectman who had entered a same-sex marriage questioned Childs's ability to provide rescue services without bias to homosexuals solely because Skip had signed the marriage petition. Skip was denied reappointment. He and his wife, who had selflessly donated hours of volunteer rescue service saving lives in their community, found they were to be punished and excluded from service. Why? Simply because they had exercised their civil rights to sign a petition protecting marriage as the union of husband and wife. That was evidence enough for the town board that Skip was an evil discriminator.

In Vermont, the owners of the Montpelier Inn, devout Catholics with eight children, were contacted by a lesbian about the possibility of holding a civil union reception at the inn. The owners never refused to hold the reception, but one of them did say that they might have a hard time putting their heart into the project because of their deeply held religious beliefs. For simply expressing this hesitation, the couple was charged with violating the state's Fair Housing and Public Accommodations Act. The inn owners have asked Liberty Counsel to represent them in the legal battle. As Matt Staver, president of Liberty Counsel, has stated, "People will use the civil union laws and same-sex 'marriage' laws to authorize the government to become 'thought police.' This case also illustrates the radical nature of the same-sex agenda."

In the last days of the 2008 campaign over Proposition 8 in California, opponents of Proposition 8 specifically targeted one religious minority, Mormons, for participating in the political process. In one particularly vile television ad campaign, a pair of Mormon missionaries was depicted ransacking the home of a lesbian couple, and Mormons were accused of trying to take over the government because they donated money and worked for the passage of Prop 8. Can you imagine the indignation (rightly so) if anyone dared to run a TV ad accusing Jews of trying to take over the government because Jewish citizens had donated "too much" money to a cause they believed in? But after the election, no less a voice than the *LA Times* editorial board actually urged gay marriage advocates to run more "hard-hitting" ads like this one.

After Prop 8 passed, gay marriage forces responded by trying to win with threats what they had lost at the ballot box: property was vandalized, artists blacklisted, worship services blocked, livelihoods threatened. Some citizens were even physically attacked because they supported marriage as the union of husband and wife.

Envelopes carrying white powder were mailed to Mormon temples in both Utah and California. Other temples were vandalized. There were public calls to "dig up dirt" on donors to "Yes on 8" and "make them pay" for daring to be involved in the political process.

The week after Prop 8 passed, pastors up and down California had to organize bodyguards in the face of threats. Police urged the pastors not to go public with the threats, for fear of generating more attempts at intimidation.

The goal of the intimidators? To make ordinary Californians afraid to speak up or to donate money for marriage as the union of husband and wife. After Prop 8, the truth is undeniable: shutting down the debate has become the modus operandi of the forces of so-called tolerance in this country.

No More Marriage

If marriage is to have any power to channel the sexual and emotional lives of the young—if it is to be a powerful norm rather than merely a set of convenient legal benefits—it must mean something.

What will marriage mean after courts redefine it? Listen to what some same-sex marriage activists say:

> I . . . believe that we may, in fact, help move the state perspective on marriage by virtue of our inclusion towards a much broader, much more capacious view. I'm thinking even of the fact of monogamy, which is both one of the pillars of heterosexual marriage and perhaps its key source of trauma. Could it be that the inclusion of lesbian and gay same-sex marriage may, in fact, sort of de-center the notion of monogamy and allow the prospect that marriage need not be an exclusive sexual relationship among people? I think it's possible.
>
> Dr. Jonathan D. Katz, founder of the Harvey Milk Institute and co-founder of Queer Nation

> [Same-sex marriage] is also a chance to wholly transform the definition of family in American culture. It is the final tool with which to dismantle all sodomy statutes, get education about homosexuality and AIDS into public

schools, and, in short, usher in a sea change in how society views and treats us.

> Michelangelo Signorile, radio
> talk show host, Sirius OutQ

By ceasing to conceive of marriage as a partnership composed of one person of each sex, the state may become more receptive to units of three or more.

> David Chambers, law professor, University of Michigan

In the polyamorist magazine *Loving More*, a journalist writing under the name of Joy Singer called for fellow polyamorists to create a civil rights movement modeled on the success of homosexual activists. First, they would campaign for basic conjugal rights such as visitation privileges in hospitals. Then they would fight for polyamorous marriage and adoption rights. Conscious of public moral disapprobation, Singer suggested that the polyamory movement select representatives acceptable to the broader public, like parents in long-term polyamorous relationships.

Here is the ACLU's current position on the issue:

> The ACLU believes that criminal and civil laws prohibiting or penalizing the practice of plural marriage violate constitutional protections of freedom of expression and association, freedom of religion, and privacy for personal relationships among consenting adults.

Not only is monogamy central to Christian morality, it is the basis of Western culture. All civil societies and all democracies have practiced monogamy. And yet as Stanley Kurtz, a fellow at the Hoover Institution and contributing editor to *National Review Online* states, "What lies beyond gay marriage is no marriage at all."

And if some activists have their way, there will be no more church either.

No More Church

A representative of a gay rights organization and an openly gay Washington state senator has reportedly stated that anyone who insists that marriage is the union between a man and a woman "should face being fined, fired, and even jailed until they relent."

Why? Why is it so important to these activists when so few even want to get married?

Same-sex marriage will make Christian teaching that sex belongs to an exclusive married union of husband and wife disfavored, legally as well as culturally. How can it be otherwise?

As I write this, activists in California are furiously denying that legalizing same-sex marriage will lead to schoolchildren being taught that same-sex marriage is a good thing. But how can they not? If the law declares same-sex marriage as sound as traditional marriage, how can public schools contradict the law?

Under same-sex marriage, Heather will have two mommies, and princes can marry other princes in the eyes of the law—and woe betide any Christian who protests. If what same-sex couples do is "marriage," then the law has made its decision. Any person, (or book, including The Book) found to utter a word of criticism against that choice would be outside the law, an exile in his or her own land.

That is what leaders of this movement want. That is what they have said they want, again and again and again. And so far they are winning.

CHAPTER SIXTEEN

"Be Angry, but Sin Not"

America will never be destroyed from the outside. If we falter and lose our freedoms, it will be because we have destroyed ourselves.

—ABRAHAM LINCOLN

In 2005, Edith Ort Thomas Elementary School in Frenchtown, New Jersey, announced that it would hold an after-school talent show called "Frenchtown Idol." Student Olivia Turton decided to participate, and she chose the song "Awesome God." When her music teacher learned what Olivia wanted to sing, she said, "Oh, that's a religious song, honey. I don't know if we can do that." The teacher did allow Olivia to rehearse but asked her for a copy of the lyrics so she could check with the principal.

> I wanted to sing that song because I am a Christian and I love God and I love singing. And I thought that song would be a good way to express how I love God.
>
> Olivia Turton, second-grade student

A couple of days after that first rehearsal, when Olivia's mother Maryann arrived at school to pick up Olivia, she found her daughter crying.

"What's the matter?" her mother asked.

"They told me I couldn't do that song," Olivia replied.

Maryann went in to speak to the principal. He referred her to the school board. The school board had ruled that Olivia could not perform the song because some of the lyrics were "questionable." One member of the school board said that the board found the song troubling not because of its religious aspects per se but because the feelings Olivia was expressing seemed to convey "that everyone else in the room should share and have those same feelings." I guess that girl can sure sell a song.

The Turtons, believing the school board's decision was unfair, contacted the Alliance Defense Fund who did agree to represent them. It took a year and a half, but the Turtons won their case. A judge ruled that the school had discriminated against Olivia because of the religious content of her expression in violation of her First Amendment rights.

That opinion is now on record, setting a precedent for other students who want to sing religious songs during after-hours school events.

Olivia's case garnered much media attention, and she was invited to sing at various events, including Revelation Generation, a popular Christian outdoor music festival held each Labor Day weekend in Frenchtown, New Jersey.†

> Now other kids get to sing songs that they want to sing, like Christian songs, in their schools, and I'm really happy about it, because I made a difference. I just hope that someone will be encouraged by my story, that they'll keep sticking up for what they believe in.
>
> Olivia Turton

A Critical Moment

In the conflict between religious liberty and sexual license, the secularists are now winning. They have every advantage of the powerful elite: the news media, Hollywood, the educational establishment, political momentum, class snobbery, and fashion, all are on their side.

This book has shown how pervasive the problem is. Now it's time to demonstrate how Christians can prevail against those who would silence us. We can defeat the powers of secular intolerance by fighting the good fight of faith.

Fight the good fight of faith, lay hold on eternal life.

1 Timothy 6:12

How can we fight back? I think there are three ways, though they overlap somewhat. First, there is the legal fight, the fight in the courtrooms. It's a fight we can't afford to lose, but it's also not going to be enough to win just this first round. Then there is the political struggle, in which I include any kind of group witness, even if politicians or elections are not involved. The boycotts we have waged against big corporations like McDonald's and our campaigns for Christmas are part of the political battle.

Finally, the most important struggle of all is the personal one: evangelization. The best thing we can do, for ourselves, for our country, is to appeal to the conscience of each person who wants to silence us. It is the best tactic because of a very simple truth: our adversaries aren't objects. They are human beings with immortal souls created in the image and likeness of God. If we speak to them, remembering who they really are, remembering that it is our job to see Christ in everyone we encounter, I think we will be shocked to realize how effective we can be. Or how effective the Spirit can be working through us.

The price of liberty is eternal vigilance, and, in America, that means having a good lawyer. Fortunately, these days Christians have some excellent lawyers.

Most Americans, and probably most Christians, don't know what rights are protected under the First Amendment. So the first thing that we need to do is to become educated as to exactly what our rights are and what recourse we have when those rights are violated.

Now several organizations are helping Christians and other people of faith in defending their religious liberty. The Alliance Defense Fund, the Rutherford Institute, the Liberty Legal Institute, the Pacific Justice Institute, Liberty Counsel, and the Becket Fund for Religious Liberty are just some of the groups that provide legal advice and other resources to people whose religious liberties have been infringed.

If you are the victim of censorship, please contact one of these organizations. If you are a Christian parent with children in public schools, please visit the Rutherford Institute's Web site at www.rutherford.org for clear and simple legal guidelines about your constitutional rights.

> Get in the courtrooms. . . . Christians have to go on the
> offensive. They have to speak truth to power like Jesus did.
> John Whitehead, president and founder,
> The Rutherford Institute,
> interview for the TV series *Speechless*

The Voice of the People

Few cities are more politically correct than Philadelphia, where we have already seen Christians silenced, and even the Boy Scouts ostracized.

Yet when that city's public schools scheduled a month of celebration in honor of gay and lesbian history, Christian parents fought back. The district planned events as "tributes to gay, lesbian, bisexual, and transgender lifestyles." A local pastor, Herb Lusk, organized hundreds of church leaders and parents, resulting in letter-writing campaigns and calls that forced the city to abandon the idea of the special observance. A school official said, "We were besieged by calls and letters, and we didn't have the manpower to staff it."†

> To make a difference, we've got to be willing to take a stand. For some, that means going to court or lobbying Congress. But for most, it's as simple as sending an e-mail or voting on Election Day or talking to your neighbors.
>
> Janet Parshall, from the TV series *Speechless*

Each and every voice made a difference. So use yours. You don't have to file a lawsuit, and you don't have to carry a picket sign to make a difference.†

Just do whatever you can in your own community. Voting is an important aspect of citizen participation in government. But it's just the first step. Remember that you are not alone. Grassroots communications can be incredibly effective, even in communities where it seems that the secularists hold all the power. Sometimes all it takes is simply spreading the word. I have been amazed over the years by how much the secularists depend on working "beneath the radar." No matter how strong they seemed and how weak we seemed in the worldly sense, in so many cases all we had to do to turn back some secularist outrage was to inform other Christians what was going on. It doesn't always work; the liberals are relentless. But it is amazing how much we can win just by staying informed.

Now I have to make an important point. Reading the stories in this book and imagining a future in which the church is silenced, it's easy to get angry. We want you to get angry. Righteous anger is not a sin, but a gift. At a certain point, Christians must fight back. Even if we are commanded to be obedient citizens, we are also commanded to follow the laws of God.

Nevertheless, be vigilant. It is very easy to stray over the line into self-righteousness. When we are self-righteous we do not follow God's law but our own; we are angry not on behalf of the truth but on behalf of ourselves. To take just one example, protesting homosexual attempts to marginalize Christians is perfectly legitimate. But carrying signs or making statements like "God Hates Homosexuals" is deeply wrong. First, it is untrue. It is proud and presumptuous. And it very likely drives sinners away from God rather than brings them closer.

The secularists want to drive religion out of politics. We should be doing just the opposite, but truly the opposite. Our faith should inform not only our opinions, but how we express them. When we go to battle we should be more Christian, not less. We should remember we are fishers of men, and we should address Christ in every man. We should hunger for converts not conquests.

This does not mean we are to be shrinking violets. But the really courageous work of the Spirit is to speak with those we disagree with forthrightly not to shout angry slogans. We have been told that we should not worry about whether we will speak well, for the Spirit will teach us what to say at the time. This means being open to the Spirit, which we cannot do if we are caught up in our own self-righteous anger, our own pride.

We don't answer defamation with defamation. But that does not mean that I cannot respond truthfully and assert the truth about what I believe. Legally speaking and in practice, the truth is the response to defamation, and Christians need to be equipped with the truth and have the courage to proclaim the truth, doing it in a respectful way but also in a way that is worthy of our Lord, to show a little bit of courage and a little bit of backbone because sometimes I think we're more afraid of the opinions of men than pleasing our Lord.

Dr. Gary L. Cass, president and CEO, Christian Anti-Defamation Commission, interview for the TV series *Speechless*

Ordinary People

The courts are one way to fight and politics and public protest are another. But the most important of all is evangelization and conversion.

First and foremost, we must evangelize each other. If Christians in this country understood the threat to their liberty and their faith, the secularists would not stand a chance. Most Christians have no idea what is at stake. Take same-sex marriage. Most Christians oppose the idea, but very few have any idea that establishing same-sex marriage along with antidiscrimination laws will make it effectively illegal to criticize the homosexual lifestyle. Most Christians have no idea that if we lose this battle we may lose our freedom to fight the next battle. The most important thing any of us can do is to spread the word of what's at stake. We all need to be Paul Reveres.

We should spread the news of the threat to our liberties. And we should spread the good news too. The good news is that Christians can be very proud of our contributions to America, both past and present. Christians have become so used to being dismissed as hateful, bigoted, or mean-spirited that they let themselves be silenced rather than fight back and speak out.

The greatest weapon our adversaries have is their ability to demoralize us. We must build the morale of Christian citizens so we can fight back.

The extent to which the media's image of Christianity is believed, even by Christians themselves, is astounding. The truth of the matter is that most of the charity in this country is performed by religious organizations and individuals. Churchgoing Christians and observant Jews lead observably less selfish and more socially productive lives than secularists. People who go to church regularly have more children, are more likely to live in families with both a mother and a father at home, and commit less crime. There is hardly a socially positive behavior that is not strongly associated with being a member of a church and attending services.

So we need to reach out to each other. Evangelization is like charity. It begins at home.

And then we need to go further, much further. In a book like this, necessarily I talk a lot about our adversaries. No way around it.

In life, though, we can't just talk about them. We need to talk to them as well. And we especially need to talk to the practicing homosexuals we know, most of whom probably aren't adversaries at all. It might be a good rule that every time we talk *about* the people we disagree with, we have to talk *to* some of them as well.

Most of us know practicing homosexuals. They can be our neighbors and colleagues, family and friends. Say you have a colleague at work. His name is Jim. He's a nice guy, a hard worker, never causes problems or makes the kinds of demands that you've read about in this book. How should you, as a concerned Christian, but also a friend, treat Jim?

First of all, Jim's homosexuality is not a problem for you to solve. You don't need to address the sins that Jim may commit in private any more than he needs to address the sins you may commit in private.

You do need to talk to him about something else.

Chances are that Jim himself doesn't realize that the leaders of the homosexual movement and the anti-Christian movement in the United States believe that a free, vigorous Christian church is something they have to eliminate, that they believe the only way to preserve their sexual liberty is to take away our religious liberty. Or maybe Jim has heard something about it, but like most people, he has never really had time to think about things from the other person's point of view.

If you want to know whether Jim supports that movement, or thinks he does, ask him some specific questions about whether he agrees with an agenda that includes silencing Christians and indoctrinating children into the homosexual lifestyle. Tell him about some of what you have learned in this book like the antibullying program, which is used as an excuse for teaching children anti-Christian propaganda and teaching young children all about homosexuality. Ask him, in all good conscience, whether he would want your child taught about homosexuality against your will? If you as a parent disagree with such programs, does he think you are a bully and a bigot?

Or tell him about corporations that sponsor gay events but treat discussion of Christian family values as hate speech. Does he think it would be a good idea for the company you both work for to allow Jim to use the company e-mail to advertise gay events but to prevent Christians from doing the same for theirs?

Tell Jim how you feel about all of this. Tell him it is your hope that he will give you as much respect for your beliefs as you do for his. Tell him that you object to your child being taught to approve what you believe as a Christian is a sin. Ask Jim to join with you to defend parents' rights in schools and see how he responds. That's a good test for Jim. Is he on the side of defending your right to raise your children as you see fit? Or is he on the side of the state supplanting your role as parent and taking over the moral education of your children?

Ask Jim these questions, and give him a chance to be as good a guy as he seems. The anti-war protestors back in the 1960s used to sing "Give Peace a Chance." Give Jim's conscience a chance. You may be pleasantly surprised at the result. And even if it does not seem to work at the time, don't despair. Sometimes when a new approach to a subject is introduced to someone, it takes a while for that person to come around.

And remember, all we have to do is talk. The Spirit will do the work.

If the religious foundations of this country are destroyed, we will lose more than just the biblical teaching on sexuality. People often seem to assume that Christian values can outlive Christianity. But that never happens. And it's not surprising, at least not to Christians. We know just how difficult it is to live up to those values, even attending church and living in a Christian family and among Christian friends.

If Christianity is discredited, so, too, will Christian charity be discredited. Do the secularists really want to live in a society where people are not taught to give to the poor and the government is the only institution that works for the public good?

Except for the most committed and aggressive secularists, very few Americans, if they knew about the stories in this book or about the implications of laws like ENDA or same-sex marriage, would say, "Ok, fine, go ahead and censor the Bible. Let the government drive Christian radio talk show hosts off the air. And take away tax exemptions from traditional churches, but not those that support liberal politicians." Most people don't go around saying, "Yes, let's persecute Christians. Yes, let's denigrate traditional families. Yes, let's allow our sexual constitution to collapse."

The problem is that most people also don't yet see that they are being faced with a choice. They don't grasp the real conflict between the secularist agenda and religious liberty or that a house divided against itself cannot stand. Most people still fall for the clever argument that says, "If we tolerate the gay lifestyle, they will go their way and we will go ours." If that were true, that would be fine. But we already know it's not true because the secularists have been shouting from the rooftops that it is not.

Any Christian who does not yet see that the secularists are out to destroy our religion hasn't been paying attention. All you have to do is listen to what the secularists say. They tell us that the conflict is real. Our obligation as Christians and as Americans is to stand up for what we believe in.

Remember, Christians, even in bitter conflict, are bound to behave in certain ways. We cannot lie about our adversaries, even when they lie about us. We cannot use the force of the state to persecute them, even if they do this to us. No amount of homosexual political agitation to silence Christians can justify gay bashing.

How do we defend ourselves against a ruthless enemy without becoming like them? It's actually not that complicated. What sometimes makes it seem complicated is that the secularists have defined tolerance as giving in to their agenda. They have defined tolerance as eliminating religion from the public square. In our time, tolerance has come to mean denying Christians any influence over the public debate. That definition will continue to expand, denying religious Americans even the right to speak on public issues. Eventually churches will be defined as public spaces, subject to government regulation, and free speech will disappear even inside the church. And because all of this is defined as tolerance and Christians are taught they must be tolerant, it can seem for a moment that there is no way we Christians can fight back and remain true to our faith.

That's wrong. Because what our opponents are asking for is not tolerance and by denying it to them we are not being intolerant. By fighting back, we are serving not only our God but also our country, conceived in liberty by Christians who knew what freedom was worth.

Our opponents and would-be oppressors are powerful, wealthy, and well organized. We will never be heard unless many voices stand up for righteousness.

Let your voice be heard. Don't be *speechless*.

NOTES

T hroughout this book's chapters you occasionally see a symbol like this one †. It signifies passages where we are using LeAnne Burnett Morse's script for the TV version of *Speechless* almost word for word, and it is only right that we recognize her excellent work.

Much of the initial research for this book was performed by the Inspiration Network during its work on *Speechless: Silencing the Christians*. Interviews by LeAnne Burnett Morse and Janet Parshall provided not only many of the quotes used in this book but also a great deal of background material and ideas. During the course of writing and revising the manuscript, we did additional research. In order for our readers (and critics) to have full access to the information that was used to write this book, we are providing research notes on each chapter.

Chapter One   Silence, Christians

Brittany McComb and John Whitehead were both interviewed by LeAnne Burnett Morse for *Speechless: Silencing the Christians* TV series. *Speechless* was co-produced by The American Family Association and INSP-The Inspiration Network, originally broadcast in fourteen half-hour episodes as a TV series and webcast on SilencingChristians.com.

Legal briefs, commentary, press releases, and video links for news programs concerning Brittany McComb's case can be found on the Web site of the Rutherford Institute, http://www.rutherford.org.

Chapter Two Why We Fight

The quote by Paula Ettelbrick came from Paula Ettelbrick, "Since When Is Marriage a Path to Liberation?" in William B. Rubenstein, ed., *Lesbians, Gay Men and the Law* (New York, NY: The New Press, 1993, pp. 401–405).

The quote by William Reich came from William Reich, "What Liberals Say," Accuracy in Media Web site, http://www.aim.org/wls/author/wilhelm-reich.

Chai Feldblum's quote originally appeared in Maggie Gallagher, "Banned in Boston—The Coming Conflict Between Same-Sex Marriage and Religious Liberty," *The Weekly Standard*, May 15, 2006, http://www.weeklystandard.com/Content/Public/Articles/000/000/012/191kgwgh.asp.

The Townhall.com columnist mentioned in this chapter is Ben Shapiro, "Mention God? Don't You Dare," Townhall.com, June 20, 2006, http://townhall.com/columnists/BenShapiro/2006/06/21/mention_god_dont_you_dare.

Franklin Kameny's quote came from Franklin Kameny, "Deconstructing the Traditional Family," *The World and I*, October 1993. (Hat tip to Alan Sears and Craig Osten.)

Jeffrey Levi's quote was found in Robert Reilly, "Culture of Vice," *National Review*, November 25, 1996.

Cathy Renna's quote was found in Marco della Cava, "Church Calls Acts 'Disordered,' Gays Feel Blamed," *USA Today*, June 12, 2002, http://www.usatoday.com/news/nation/2002/06/12/acov-usat.htm.

Chai Feldblum's quote came from Chai Feldblum, "The 'Gay Agenda'," *Advocate*, July 11, 2003, http://www.planetout.com/news/feature.html?sernum=604.

The Homosexual Agenda is available online at the American Family Association Web site, http://www.afa.net/Homosexual_Agenda/ha1972.htm.

The details of the Gay Rights Platform was described in Eugene Volokh, "Same-Sex Marriage and Slippery Slopes," *Hofstra Law Review* 33:1155–1201 (2005).

Chapter Three   The Bully of the Schoolyard

The opening quote from the American Civil Liberties Union was from Alan Sears and Craig Osten's, *The ACLU vs. America: Exposing the Agenda to Redefine Moral Values* (Nashville: TN, B & H Publishing Group, 2005, p. 57).

Hillary Clinton's quote came from Martha Brant and Evan Thomas, "First Fighter," *Newsweek*, 1996, http://www.newsweek.com/id/34610.

The *Guide* quote was found in *Traditional Values Coalition, Exposed, Homosexual Child Molesters* online brochure, Traditional Values Coalition Web site, http://www.traditionalvalues.org/pdf_files/HomosexualChildMolestersUrban.pdf.

Much of the information on the Boyd County case came from the Alliance Defense Fund. Legal documents, news articles, and press releases concerning Boyd County and other related cases can be found on the ADF Web site, http://www.alliancedefensefund.org.

The "Myth and Facts" section of the curriculum and the video transcript of the training film were quoted from legal documents provided by the ADF.

Tim, Mary, and T. J. Morrison were interviewed by LeAnne Burnett Morse for the *Speechless* TV series. Their case was *Morrison v. Board of Education of Boyd County*, 521 F.3d 602 (6th Cir. 2008).

The *Making Schools Safe Training Manual* is available from the ACLU Web site, http://www.aclu.org/lgbt/youth/24003pub 20060131.html.

The controversy over the Evesham School District was covered in Troy Graham, "Same Sex Diversity Video Roils Evesham District," *Philadelphia Inquirer*, January 24, 2007, B4, http://www.philly.com/philly/news/5339146.html.

An invaluable resource for the writing of this chapter was The Family Research Council, *Homosexuality in Your Child's School*, Family Research Council online brochure, http://www.frc.org/get.cfm?i=BC06D02. Several of the instances of school programs and curricula were taken from that source, as well as quoted material regarding the song "In Mommy's High Heels," from the theatrical production *Cootie Shots*.

Another helpful resource was Sears and Osten, *The Homosexual Agenda: Exposing the Principal Threat to Religious Freedom Today* (Nashville, TN: B & H Publishing Group, 2003). This book provided the quote from the film *It's Elementary*, as well as the quote that begins, "You may come to the conclusion . . ."

Up-to-date (at press time) information on "safe schools" programs in different states came from The Gay, Lesbian and Straight Education Network, "2007 National School Climate Survey," *The Gay, Lesbian and Straight Education Network Executive Summary*, October 2008, http://www.glsen.org/binary-data/GLSEN_ATTACHMENTS/file/000/001/1306-1.pdf.

Useful background material and the reference to "A lesbian state senator from California . . ." introducing SB 777 came from the Campaign for Children and Families Web site, http://www.savecalifornia.com/getpluggedin/news_details.php?newsid=71. Another source for this material was the 2007 California Senate Bill 777 (as introduced).

The reference to "a lesson plan for kindergartners in San Francisco . . ." was quoted from Debra Saunders, "Gay-Ed for Tots," *The Weekly Standard*, August 19, 1996.

The reference to "The state of Maryland has put itself . . ." came from court documents provided by the Alliance Defense

Fund. The story is also covered in Daniel de Vise's "Maryland State Board Approves County's Sex-Ed Curriculum," *The Washington Post*, July 4, 2007, B6.

Information on the Massachusetts public schools came from Sears and Osten, *The Homosexual Agenda: Exposing the Principal Threat to Religious Freedom Today* (Nashville, TN: B & H Publishing Group, 2003) and the Family Research Council, *Homosexuality in Your Child's School*, Family Research Council online brochure, http://www.frc.org/get.cfm?i=BC06D02.

The quote from the author of *Who's in a Family?* came from an interview with Robert Skutch on National Public Radio's program *Here and Now*, originally aired on May 3, 2005. It was also cited in Baldwin and Holgate, *From Crayons to Condoms* (Los Angeles, CA: WND Books, 2008, p. 153).

Katherine Kersten's column of May 11, 2008, which I quoted with permission from the *Star Tribune*, titled "The real agenda behind schools' anti-bullying curricula," can also be found online at http://www.startribune.com/local/18846129.html.

Kevin Jennings's comments about the Massachusetts Governor's Commission on Gay and Lesbian Youth were taken from the article "Governor's Commission for 'Gay Youth' Retreats to 'Safety' and 'Suicide,'" *Massachusetts News*, December 2000, http://www.massnews.com/past_issues/2000/12_Dec/1200fist3.htm.

Dr. Gary Cass was interviewed by Janet Parshall for the *Speechless: Silencing the Christians* TV series. The NEA "Diversity Resolution" was described and discussed in Phyllis Schlafly, "The NEA Spells Out Its Policies," Townhall.com, July 28, 2008, http://townhall.com/Columnists/PhyllisSchlafly/2008/07/28/the_nea_spells_out_its_policies.

The California law affecting interscholastic sports refers to SB 225, which would require interscholastic sports teams to adopt nondiscrimination codes supporting "sexual orientation" as well as "perceived gender" or risk being banned from the California Interscholastic Federation.

Chapter Four   The ACLU v. The U.S. Constitution

The first book anyone should read about the ACLU is Alan Sears and Craig Osten's *The ACLU vs. America: Exposing the Agenda to Redefine Moral Values* (Nashville, TN: B & H Publishing Group, 2005). This book was instrumental in providing background research and specific quotes for this chapter. It was also an ample primary source for material that we might not have discovered without having it as a resource.

Several of the Pattison Elementary parents and students were interviewed by LeAnne Burnett Morse. Some wished not to be quoted by name, and we have honored that request. Research on the Katy School District was provided by Kelly Shackleford, chief counsel for Liberty Legal Institute, who was also interviewed by LeAnne Burnett Morse. Shackleford is affiliated with Liberty Legal, which provided both court records and primary documents from the school system itself. The problems in the Texas schools were first brought to many people's attention by David Limbaugh, *Persecution: How Liberals are Waging War Against Christianity* (Washington, DC: Regnery, 2003).

Information on the Plano School District cases was provided by Kelly Shackleford. John Gibson also wrote extensively about the Plano schools in his book *The War on Christmas: How the Liberal Plot to Ban the Sacred Christian Holiday is Worse than You Thought* (New York, NY: Sentinel, 2005).

Thomas Jefferson's letter to the Danbury Baptist Association was found at the Library of Congress Web site, http://www.loc.gov/loc/lcib/9806/danpre.html.

Supreme Court Justice Brennan's articulation of "strict scrutiny" was found in *Sherbert v. Verner*, 374 U.S. 398 (1963).

Antonin Scalia's quote about religious speech came from *Capitol Square Review & Advisory Board v. Pinette*, 515 U.S. 753, 760 (1995).

The quote from John Whitehead of the Rutherford Institute, "Taxpayers have to pay for . . ." came from his interview with LeAnne Burnett Morse.

Kelly Coghlan was interviewed by LeAnne Burnett Morse, and he kindly provided us with supporting documents, including a copy of the Texas law that he helped draft.

Chapter Five   Some Religions Are More Equal than Others

The opening quote from the sheik's sermon at Sidon Mosque on February 13, 2004, was cited in Jamie Tarabay, "Australia Muslim Leader Defends His Anti-Israel Attacks," *Jerusalem Post*, March 11, 2004, p. 5.

Brad Dacus of the Pacific Justice Institute was interviewed by LeAnne Burnett Morse. More information about PJI's efforts to fight Muslim indoctrination in our public schools was found on their Web site, http://www.pacificjustice.org/resources/articles/focus.cfm?ID=ART434511306.

Excerpts from *Across the Centuries* (Boston, MA: Houghton Mifflin School, 2002) and the Muslim "simulation" student guide were found on the BlessedCause Web site, http://www.blessed-cause.org. However, the quotes from *Across the Centuries* cited in this chapter were taken directly from the textbook itself.

The erasure of our Christian heritage from school textbooks was described in Ellen Sorokin, "No Founding Fathers? That's our New History," *The Washington Times*, January 28, 2002. Paul C. Vitz, *Censorship: Evidence of Bias in Our Children's Textbooks*

(Ann Arbor, MI: Servant Books, 1986) was also a source for this chapter. Both authors' works were cited in David Limbaugh, *Persecution: How Liberals Are Waging War Against Christianity* (Washington, DC: Regnery, 2003).

More information on the fight to defend the rights of students and parents against Muslim indoctrination can be found at The Thomas More Law Center's Web site, http://www.thomasmore.org.

The controversy at Carver Elementary was detailed in "Islamic Prayers Finally Dropped," *WorldNetDaily* online magazine, August 1, 2007, http://www.worldnetdaily.com/news/article.asp? ARTICLE_ID=56945.

The reference to Kahlil Gibran and Muslim public schools in America was extensively covered on Daniel Pipes's Web site, http://www.danielpipes.org/category.

The University of North Carolina at Chapel Hill's required reading of the Koran was reported in the late Reed Irvine's " Required Reading of the Koran Contested," Accuracy in Media Web site, July 24, 2002, http://www.aim.org/publications/ weekly_column/2002/07/24.html.

FIRE's (Foundation for Individual Rights in Education) Web site is an excellent resource for students, parents, educators, and anyone interested in the state of religious freedom in American colleges and universities, http://www.thefire.org.

Ihsan Bagby's quote has been widely cited. The version quoted here came from Joe Kaufman, "Department of the Defenseless," *FrontPage* online magazine, January 28, 2008, http://www.frontpagemag.com/Articles/Read.aspx?GUID=AE1AE743-9F2B-448A-BCF4-2D702EC6844C. Another version was found in Joel Mowbray, "The House that Raised Akbar," *National Review Online*, April 3, 2003, http://www.nationalreview.com/mowbray/ mowbray040303.asp.

Donna Busch and John Whitehead of the Rutherford Institute were both interviewed by LeAnne Burnett Morse. Additional information came from legal documents provided by the Rutherford Institute and available on their Web site, http://www.rutherford.org. The case citation is *Busch v. Marple Newtown School District*, 2007 WL 1589507 (E.D. Pa. 2007).

Chapter Six   Leviathan v. The Boy Scouts

The opening quote came from Jim DeMint and J. David Woodward, *Why We Whisper: Restoring our Right to Say It's Wrong* (Lanham, MD: Rowman & Littlefield, 2008). This book was not only useful for up-to-date research but also stimulated several important ideas. It covers both the anti-Christian prejudice experienced by both authors and other related cases, and it makes a strong argument for concerned Christians to speak up.

Vietnam War veteran Joseph Kinney was interviewed by Leanne Burnett Morse.

The American Family Association's Action Alert detailing the AFA's fight to restore the flag-folding ceremony at Christian burials by the Veterans Affairs Department was found at the AFA Web site, https://secure.afa.net/afa/activism/TakeAction.asp?id=270.

The AFA Action Alert concerning the National Park Service's attempts to censor God from the Washington Monument was found at the AFA Web site, https://secure.afa.net/afa/activism/TakeAction.asp?id=271.

The story of the Philadelphia Boy Scouts was based on several different sources:

Hans Zieger, "Philly's Cold Shoulder," *The Washington Times* online, January 22, 2008, http://www.washingtontimes.com/news/2008/jan/22/phillys-cold-shoulder/.

Gudrun Schultz, "Philly City Council Ends 79-Year Boy Scout Lease Over Refusal to Accept Homosexual Leaders," *LifeSiteNews* online magazine, June 1, 2007, http://www.lifesite-news.com/ldn/2007/jun/07060104.html.

Catherine Donaldson-Evans, "Boy Scouts' Rent Skyrockets in Philadelphia to $200K Over Gay Ban," *Fox News* online, October 19, 2007, http://www.foxnews.com/story/0,2933,303420,00.html.

Chad Groening, "Boy Scout Advocate Calls on Americans to Boycott Philadelphia," Do The Right Thing Web Site, October 25, 2007, http://dotherightthing-cyberpastor.blogspot.com/2007/10/boy-scout-advocate-calls-on-americans.html.

"Boy Scouts Ignore 'Pay-Up-Or-Move' Ultimatum," *WorldNetDaily* online magazine, December 14, 2007, http://www.worldnetdaily.com/news/article.asp?ARTICLE_ID=59021.

Stefan Kanfer's quote came from his article, "Why the Scouts Ban Homosexuals," *City Journal*, Winter 2002, http://www.city-journal.org/html/12_1_sndgs12.html.

The full citation for U.S. Supreme Court Chief Justice Rehnquist's majority opinion came from *Boy Scouts of America v. Dale*, 530 U.S. 640 (2000) quoting *Hurley v. Irish American Gay, Lesbian, and Bisexual Group of Boston*, 515 U.S. 557 (1995), http://caselaw.lp.findlaw.com/scripts/getcase.pl?navby=CASE&court=US&vol=530&page=640#section1.

The story of the ACLU's battle to keep the Boy Scout Jamboree off U.S. Army bases was recounted in "Boy Scout Jamboree to Stay at Army Base," *The Washington Times*, November 16, 2004, http://www.washingtontimes.com/news/2004/nov/16/20041116-115229-4427r/.

Another source was "Pentagon Agrees to End Direct Sponsorship of Boy Scout Troops in Response to Religious Discrimination Charge," ACLU Press Release, November 15, 2004, http://www.aclu.org/religion/discrim/16382prs20041115.html.

Various state and civic efforts to limit Boy Scout activities were described in these sources:

Kate Zernike, "Scouts' Successful Ban on Gays Is Followed by Loss in Support," *The New York Times*, August 29, 2000, http://query.nytimes.com/gst/fullpage.html?res=9405E4DF1F31 F93AA1575BC0A9669C8B63.

Lambda Legal, "The Impact of the Boy Scouts of America's Anti-Gay Discrimination," Lambda Legal Web Site, September 24, 2003, http://www.lambdalegal.org/our-work/publications/facts-backgrounds/page.jsp?itemID=31989419.

Sara Rimer, "Boy Scouts Under Fire," *The New York Times*, July 3, 2003, http://query.nytimes.com/gst/fullpage.html?res= 9A05E4D6103AF930A35754C0A9659C8B63&sec=&spon=&pa gewanted=2.

Boy Scouts of America spokesman Gregg Shields was quoted in Ian Urbina, "Boy Scouts Lose Philadelphia Lease in Gay-Rights Fight," *The New York Times*, December 6, 2007, http://www. nytimes.com/2007/12/06/us/06scouts.html.

Terry Phillis was quoted in Bob Unruh, "Boy Scouts' Banishment Threatens Catholic Church," by *WorldNetDaily* online magazine, December 14, 2007, http://www.worldnetdaily.com/ index.php?fa=PAGE.view&pageId=45059.

Chuck Colson was interviewed by Janet Parshall.

The quote from Barry Lynn, "It is unconstitutional and morally wrong . . ." and the quote from Mark Earley came from David Bohon, "Faith-based Mentoring Program Facing Liberal Lawsuit," Minnesota Family Council Web site, January 28, 2008, http://www.mfc.org/contents/article.cfm?id=1517.

The quote from Barry Lynn "a very long, deep shadow . . ." originally appeared in William Petroski, "Court: State Can't Pay for Religious Prison Treatment," *Des Moines Register*, December 3, 2007.

Chapter Seven   **The New Persecutors**

The opening quote came from Robert Reilly, "Culture of Vice," *National Review*, November 25, 1996. Marshall K. Kirk and Hunter Madsen's quote came from their book, *After the Ball: How America Will Conquer Its Fear and Hatred of Gays in the 90's* (New York, NY: Plume, 1990).

The story of the "Philadelphia 11" came from interviews with members of Repent America, from video taken during the event, from documents of the group's various legal proceedings, and from a host of news articles, particularly *WorldNetDaily* on-line magazine, which has an entire series on the Philadelphia 11 on their Web site. An article re. Michael Marcavage with links to the series is: Bob Unruh, "Philly 'gay'-fest protester's free-speech case revived," *WorldNetDaily* online magazine, April 02, 2008, http://www.worldnetdaily.com/index.php?fa=PAGE.view&pageId=60548.

The anecdote concerning the Madison, Wisconsin, fireman came from Sears and Osten, *The Homosexual Agenda: Exposing the Principal Threat to Religious Freedom Today* (Nashville, TN: B & H Publishing Group, 2003, p. 157).

The anecdote about condoms in a Colorado church came from Rosemary Harris, "Church Service Is Interrupted by Gay Activists Throwing Condoms," *Colorado Springs Gazette-Telegraph*, November 8, 1993.

The disruption of the "Love Won Out" conference was detailed in Robert Knight and Lindsey Douthit's "'Hate Crime' Laws Threaten Religious Freedom," Concerned Women for America Web site, December 12, 2005, http://www.cwfa.org/articledisplay.asp?id=9672&department=CFI&categoryid=papers.

Examples of the San Francisco Police Department refusing to protect Christians are cited in Sears and Osten, *Homosexual Agenda: Exposing the Principal Threat to Religious Freedom Today*

(Nashville, TN: B & H Publishing Group, 2003, p. 158) and on the Christian Anti-Defamation Commission Web site, http://www.christianadc.org/pages/page.asp?page_id=23073&articleId=1198. The Web site also recounts various episodes of blasphemy, persecution, and harassment of Christians in the city of San Francisco.

The story of the Dayton, Tennessee, men arrested for erecting wooden crosses was told in Sears and Osten, *Homosexual Agenda: Exposing the Principal Threat to Religious Freedom Today* (Nashville, TN: B & H Publishing Group, 2003, p. 159).

San Francisco's Folsom Street Fair poster is described in "Folsom Street 'Last Supper Ad' Sparks Controversy," at KTVU.com, http://www.ktvu.com/news/14227320/detail.html.

The Christian Anti-Defamation Commission URL above was also the source for the note left by Matthew Murray prior to his shooting spree.

Dr. Gary Cass was interviewed by Janet Parshall.

Chapter Eight   The Children of this World

The opening quote was found on the Alliance Defense Fund Web Site's online brochure titled, *The Most Serious Threat to Your Religious Freedom*, http://www.alliancedefensefund.org/issues/traditionalfamily/default.aspx?cid=4429. This quote was originally cited by Sears and Osten, *Homosexual Agenda: Exposing the Principal Threat to Religious Freedom Today* (Nashville, TN: B & H Publishing Group, 2003, p. 165).

David Gibbs's quote, as well as the full story of Matt Barber's termination came from Ron Strom, "[Major Fortune 100 Company] Terminates Manager Over Homosexuality Column," *WorldNetDaily* online magazine, June 24, 2005.

Trish Mehaffey reported on "Ex-employee sues Rockwell,

Claims Religious Discrimination," in the *Cedar Rapids Gazette*, May 17, 2008, http://www.gazetteonline.com/apps/pbcs.dll/article?AID=/20080517/NEWS/444749614/1006/news.

General Motors' prohibition of a Christian employee network was cited in David Limbaugh, *Persecution: How Liberals Are Waging War Against Christianity* (Washington, DC: Regnery, 2003, p. 372). Several of the other anecdotes in this chapter came from the Family Research Council, *The Other Side of Tolerance—How Homosexual Activism Threatens Liberty*, Family Research Council online brochure, http://www.frc.org/get.cfm?i=BC06H02.

Another important source for these anecdotes was Robert Knight, "The Corporate Curtain: How Companies Are Using Views on Homosexuality to Punish their Christian Employees," January 20, 2006, Concerned Women for America Web site, http://www.cwfa.org/articles/9808/CFI/papers/index.htm.

An additional source was Philippe Naughton, "Christians Urged to Boycott Co-op After Bank Row," *Times Online* Web site, June 24, 2005, http://timesonline.co.uk/tol/news/uk/article536900.ece.

"More than half of the Fortune 500 companies . . ." came from Stephanie Armour, "Gay Parents Cheer a Benefit Revolution," *USA Today*, January 10, 2005, 1B, http://www.usatoday.com/money/workplace/2005-01-09-gay-parents_x.htm.

The city of San Francisco's policies were described in Christopher Heredia, "Equal Benefit Law in S.F. Has Big Impact Across U.S.," *San Francisco Chronicle*, November 4, 2001, A23, http://links.sfgate.com/cgi-bin/article.cgi?f=/c/a/2001/11/04/MN186395.DTL&hw=equaled&sn=032&sc=254.

Brian McNaught was quoted in Robert Knight, "Sexual Orientation and American Culture," Concerned Women for America Web site, July 10, 2002, http://www.cwfa.org/articledisplay.asp?id=2927&department=CFI&categoryid=papers.

Elizabeth Birch was quoted in Robert Knight, "The Corporate

Curtain: How Companies are Using Views on Homosexuality to Punish Their Christian Employees," Concerned Women for America Web site, January 20, 2006, http://www.cwfa.org/articledisplay.asp?id=9808&department=CFI&categoryid=papers.

The reference to "The radical homosexual agenda" came from Sears and Osten, *Homosexual Agenda: Exposing the Principal Threat to Religious Freedom Today* (Nashville, TN: B & H Publishing Group, 2003, p. 179).

Robert Knight's quote was cited in Erin Curry, "Starbucks Promotes Homosexual Agenda with Coffee Cup," *Baptist Press* online magazine, August 12, 2005, http://www.bpnews.net/BPnews.asp? ID=21387.

Donations from Peter Lewis to the ACLU were reported in "$8 Million Gift Will Boost ACLU Campaign to Fight Bush Administration's Assault on Civil Liberties," ACLU Press Release, November 15, 2003, http://www.aclu.org/about/support/13308prs20030115.html.

Starbucks' policies were described in Meghan Kleppinger, "Starbucks: A Habit Easily Broken," *WorldNetDaily* online magazine, August 10, 2005, http://www.worldnetdaily.com/index.php?pageId=31716.

Disney's pro-homosexual policies were described in Ross van Metzke, "Gay Days at Disneyland Part Celebration, Part Fiasco," *Advocate* online magazine, October 6, 2008, http://www.advocate.com/exclusive_detail_ektid63116.asp. Another reference was Loann Halden, "For a Day or Two, It's the Gayest Place On Earth," *Miami Herald*, May 11, 2008, J10, http://miamiherald.typepad.com/gaysouthflorida/2008/05/magic-kingdom-f.html.

The kingdombuy.com story was told in "Enterprise Rent-A-Car, J. Crew Spurn Online Christian Business," *AFA Journal* online magazine, August 2001, http://www.afa.net/journal/august/internet.asp.

You can learn more about the campaign against Cracker Barrel from Rusty Pugh and Jody Brown, "Pro Family Group: Restaurant Chain Cracks Under Pressure from Homosexual Activists," *Agape Press*, December 9, 2002, http://headlines.agapepress.org/archive/12/afa/92002a.asp.

The McDonald's controversy was recounted in Kathleen Gilbert, "Boycott Successful: McDonald's Abandons Homosexual Activism," *LifeSiteNews* online magazine, October 10, 2008, www.lifesitenews.com/ldn/2008/oct/08/01003.htm.

Michael Medved's quote came from Michael Medved, "Fact or Fiction," Alliance Defense Fund Web site, Document2http://www.alliancedefensefund.org/adfresources/faq.aspx?cid=3212.

The percentage of homosexuals in America came from Robert T. Michael, John H. Gagnon, Edward Laumann, and Gina Kolata, *Sex in America: A Definitive Survey* (New York, NY: Warner Books, 1995).

Chapter Nine   Whose Birthday Is It, Anyway?

John Whitehead's quote came from his interview with LeAnne Burnett Morse for the TV series *Speechless*.

All of the material concerning the Becket Fund's efforts to preserve Christmas traditions came from that organization's Web site: http://www.becketfund.org.

Nadine Strossen's statement came from "The Real Christmas Spirit," ACLU Newsletter, November 1998, found in Sears and Osten, *The ACLU vs. America: Exposing the Agenda to Redefine Moral Values* (Nashville, TN: B & H Publishing Group, 2005, p. 162).

The author's quote was from John Gibson, *The War on Christmas: How the Liberal Plot to Ban the Sacred Christian Holiday is Worse than You Thought* (New York, NY: Sentinel, 2005, p. 189). This book is the single best-printed source on the topic. (The best electronic source, of course, is the AFA Web site: http://www.afa.net.)

Other useful information about the war against Christmas came from David Limbaugh, *Persecution: How Liberals Are Waging War Against Christianity* (Washington, DC: Regnery, 2003).

Chapter Ten   The IRS Inquisition

The quote from Michael Schwartz came from Michael Schwartz, "Houses of Worship Free Speech Restoration Act," Concerned Women for America Web site, March 26, 2003, http://www.cwfa.org/articles/3628/CWA/freedom/index.htm.

A fact sheet telling the full story about Canyon Ferry Road Baptist Church was found on the Alliance Defense Fund Web site, http://www.telladf.org/UserDocs/CanyonFerryFactSheet.pdf.

Details of the Internal Revenue Code and case law concerning tax-exempt organizations are outlined in "IRS 'Preacher Police' Retreat Welcomed," FreePreach.org Web site, September 24, 2007, http://www.FreePreach.org.

Another useful source was Brendan Miniter, "Bullying the Pulpits: The IRS threatens church leaders who talk about politics," published in *The Wall Street Journal*, March 10, 2006, from which Mark Everson's quote was taken, www.freepreach.org/index.php/article/485.html?PHPSESSID=ed3178663ae7596e49bd0e1ccf742dc4.

Don Alexander's quote originally appeared in John Berlau, "Churches Must Follow IRS Gospel," *Insight* online magazine, October 22, 2001, http://www.theforbiddenknowledge.com/hardtruth/irs_rules_churches.htm.

The *Wall Street Journal* editorial came from "The Taxman Goes to Church," *The Wall Street Journal*, August 25, 2006, http://www.opinionjournal.com/taste/?id=110008841.

The travails of the Church at Pierce Creek in Vestal, NY, were recounted in Julie Foster, "Church Loses Tax-Exempt Status:

Organization Had Placed Newspaper Ads Criticizing Bill Clinton," *WorldNetDaily* online magazine, May 13, 2000, http://www.worldnetdaily.com/index.php?pageId=4497.

Dr. James Dobson was quoted from Dr. James Dobson's "Focus on the Family Withstands Liberal Group's Attack," *Focus on the Family Newsletter*, October 2007, http://www2.focusonthefamily.com/docstudy/newsletters/A000000953.cfm.

David Limbaugh's quote came from *Persecution: How Liberals Are Waging War Against Christianity* (Washington, DC: Regnery, 2003, p. 213).

To see how your U.S. state representatives voted on the Houses of Worship Political Speech Protection Act in 2003, go to http://www.highbeam.com/doc/1G1-94335113.html.

Chapter Eleven   The UnFairness Doctrine

The opening quote came from Wendy Schibener, "Pence Needs 23 More Signatures," Human Events.com, June 19, 2008, http://www.humanevents.com/article.php?id=27085.

James Gattuso of the Heritage Foundation was interviewed by Janet Parshall. That interview not only provided the quotes attributed to Gattuso but also a great deal of background material and ideas concerning the Fairness Doctrine. Another good source was Byron York, "An Unfair Doctrine," *National Review* 59, July 30, 2007, p. 32.

The quote from Bill Ruder was found in Lucas A. Powe Jr.'s *American Broadcasting and the First Amendment* (Berkeley: University of California Press, 1987, p. 115), courtesy of Brian Fitzpatrick, senior editor, *Unmasking the Myths Behind the Fairness Doctrine, Executive Summary from the Culture and Media Institute, 2008.* This report was also a great resource for understanding the history of the Fairness Doctrine and the threats posed by its possible reinstatement, http://www.cultureandmediainstitute.org/ specialreports/2008/Fairness_Doctrine/FairnessDoctrine_Full- Report.htm.

The "Structural Imbalance in Political Talk Radio" study came from John Halpin et al., *The Structural Imbalance of Political Talk Radio, A Joint Report by the Center for American Progress and Free Press*, June 21, 2007, updated June 22, 2007, http://www. americanprogress.org/pressroom/releases/2007/06/radio_re- lease.html.

Nancy Pelosi's quote to the *Christian Science Monitor* was cited in John Gizzi's, "Pelosi Supports 'Fairness Doctrine,'" Human Events.com, June 25, 2008, http://www.humanevents.com/arti- cle.php?id=27185.

Further information is available in Vivian Nereim, "Will De- mocrats Hush Rush?" *Pittsburgh Post-Gazette*, July 13, 2008, A1, http://www.post-gazette.com/pg/08195/896760-176.stm.

The article "Her Royal Fairness" in *The American Spectator*, May 2007, was written by "The Washington Prowler," http://www.spectator.org/archives/2007/05/14/her-royal- fairness.

Sen. Durbin's quote, "It's time to reinstitute . . ." was found in Alexander Bolton, "GOP Preps for Talk Radio Confrontation," *The Hill*, June 27, 2007, http://thehill.com/leading-the- news/gop-preps-for-talk-radio-confrontation-2007-06-27.html. His further comments were from Frederic J. Frommer, "Democ- rats Block Amendment to Prevent Fairness Doctrine," The Asso- ciated Press, July 14, 2007.

Reference to Dennis Kucinich by a staffer also came from "Her Royal Fairness."

Statistics on media proliferation and diversity came from Adam D. Thierer, "The Media Cornucopia," *City Journal*, Spring 2007, http://www.city-journal.org/html/17_2_media.html.

Chapter Twelve   **The ENDA Agenda**

Hallinan's quote was from Sears and Osten, *Homosexual Agenda: Exposing the Principal Threat to Religious Freedom Today* (Nashville, TN: B & H Publishing Group, 2003, p. 215).

The dates and authors of the discussed articles in the *Toledo Free Press* were cited in the text. Crystal Dixon's press conference was covered by Meghan Gilbert, "Dixon Says University of Toledo Termination violated free speech," *The Toledo Blade*, May 15, 2008, http://www.toledoblade.com/apps/pbcs.dll/article?AID=/20080515/NEWS21/805150352.

The Family Research Council's comment first appeared in "Holy Toledo! Ohio Employee Suspended for Voicing Her Values," *FRC Action Washington Update* electronic newsletter, May 6, 2008, http://www.frcaction.org/get.cfm?i=WU08E03.

The quote "seeks to chill . . ." and other important background information that proved helpful throughout this chapter were provided by Robert H. Knight and Kenneth L. Ervin II, "Talking Points: The Employment Non-Discrimination Act," Concerned Women For America Web site, February 27, 2002, http://www.cultureandfamily.org/articledisplay.asp?id=2578&department=CFI&categoryid=papers.

Statistics on state and city discrimination laws were found in the Human Rights Campaign, "Human Rights Campaign, Employment Non-Discrimination Laws on Sexual Orientation and Gender Identity," Human Rights Campaign Web site, http://www.hrc.org/issues/4844.htm.

The reference to "Doctors are being successfully sued for not performing artificial insemination . . ." was based on *North Coast Women's Care Medical Group, Inc. v. San Diego County Superior Court*, S 142892, Ct. App. 4/1 DO4543881 (August 18, 2008), http://www.courtinfo.ca.gov/opinions/documents/S142892.PDF.

The reference to "A licensed counselor was fired . . ." came from the article "Counselor Fired After Referring Homosexual to Colleague Because of Religious Beliefs," *LifeSiteNews* online magazine, July 17, 2008, http://www.lifesitenews.com/ldn/2008/jul/08071717.html.

The story of video technician and small business owner Tim Bono was told in Robert Knight, "Christian Business Ordered to Duplicate Homosexual Activist Videos," Concerned Women for America Web site, April 25, 2006, http://www.cwfa.org/articles/10594/CFI/family/index.htm.

The announcement of the decision to drop the case against Bono was made in an Arlington County online news release titled "Arlington County Human Rights Commission Dismisses Discrimination Case Against Video Store Owner: Reaffirms Protection Afforded to all Persons from Discriminatory Acts," County of Arlington News Release, June 10, 2006, http://www.arlingtonva.us/Departments/Communications/PressReleases/5445.aspx.

Al Gore's comment on the Boy Scouts was made on *Good Morning America* during an interview with Charles Gibson on October 26, 2000, and it is cited in Robert H. Knight and Kenneth L. Ervin II, "Talking Points: The Employment Non-Discrimination Act," Concerned Women For America Web site, February 27, 2007, http://www.cultureandfamily.org/articledisplay.asp?id=2578&department=CFI&categoryid=papers.

California's definition of gender came from Senate Bill 777, signed into law by Gov. Schwarzenegger on October 12, 2007.

Gavin Newsom's, Bishop Andrew Merritt's, and Rev. Jesse Jackson's quotes on civil rights were found in Cheryl Wetzstein, "Blacks Angered by Gays' Metaphors," *The Washington Times*, March 1, 2004, p. 3, and in a Family Research Council brochure, *The Slippery Slope of Same-Sex 'Marriage'*, Family Research Council Web site, http://www.frc.org/get.cfm?i=bc04c02.

Quote from Bishop Harry Jackson came from Harry R. Jackson Jr., "Time to End ENDA," TownHall.com, October 23, 2007, http://townhall.com/columnists/HarryRJacksonJr/2007/10/23/time_to_end_enda.

The full text of demands from the 1987 National March on Washington for Lesbian and Gay Rights was found on the American Family Association Web site, http://www.afa.net/homosexual_agenda/ha1987.htm.

Dr. James Dobson's comments on the Colorado law came from "Dr. Dobson Decries Ritter's Signing of SB 200," Focus on the Family Press Release, May 30, 2008, http://www2.focusonthefamily.com/press/pressreleases/A000001170.cfm.

The story about DignityUSA in Minneapolis was based on *Dignity Twin Cities v. Newman Center & Chapel*, 472 NW2d 355 (Minn. App. 1991), http://www.danpinello.com/Dignity.htm.

Chapter Thirteen   The Gospel of Hate

The opening quote came from Robert Knight and Lindsey Douthit, "'Hate Crimes Laws Threaten Religious Freedom," Concerned Women for America Web site, December 12, 2005, http://www.cwfa.org/articledisplay.asp?id=9672&department=cfi&categoryid=papers. This document was also useful in providing background information on the issue of hate crimes laws and for examples of how these laws have been applied, both in the United States and elsewhere. The Concerned Women for America Web site (http://www.cwfa.org) has this article and several other useful articles on the topic.

The story of the Good News Employee Association is told in Bob Unruh, "'N-word' Fine, but 'Family Values' Banned: Christians Challenge Ruling that 'Hate Speech' Could Spare Workers," *WorldNetDaily* online magazine, June 5, 2007, http://www.

worldnetdaily.com/news/article.asp?ARTICLE_ID=56013.
Quotes in this section came from that article and from legal documents.

The quote by Jan LaRue, the citations from the proposed federal legislation, and the statistics on reported hate crimes in California all came from Robert Knight, "The Federal Hate Crimes Bill: Federalizing Criminal Law While Threatening Civil Liberties," Concerned Women for America Web site, September 29, 2005, http://www.cwfa.org/articledisplay.asp?id=9069&department=CFI&categoryid=papers.

Senator Edward M. Kennedy's quote was originally published in Adam Clymer, "Senate Panel Moves to Block Bias Against Gays at Work," *The New York Times*, April 25, 2002, A26, http://query.nytimes.com/gst/fullpage.html?res=9E07EFD8143 EF936A15757C0A9649C8B63.

The reference "One federal bill in consideration . . ." was to Local Law Enforcement Hate Crimes Prevention Act of 2007 (HR1592).

The story about Traverse, Michigan, was reported in David Limbaugh, *Persecution: How Liberals Are Waging War Against Christianity* (Washington, DC: Regnery, 2003, p. 244).

Matt Foreman's quote came from the National Gay and Lesbian Task Force, "Task Force Calls Rise in Anti-Gay Crime a Product of America's Anti-Gay Industry," National Gay and Lesbian Task Force Press Release, April 26, 2005, http://www.thetaskforce.org/press/releases/pr815_042605.

The incidents of staged hate crimes were recounted in Lindsey Douthit, "For Real: Many Well-Publicized 'Hate Crimes' Were Staged," Concerned Women for America Web site, August 24, 2005, http://www.cwfa.org/articles/8776/CFI/family/index.htm.

Robert Knight's quote concerning hate crimes being mostly acts of speech came from Robert Knight, "'Hate Crime' Laws: An

Assault on Freedom," Concerned Women for America Web site, September 27, 2005, http://www.cwfa.org/articles/2575/CFI/ papers/index.htm.

Rev. Bob Schenk's anecdote about the Supreme Court came from Robert Knight, "The Federal Hate Crimes Bill: Federalizing Criminal Law While Threatening Civil Liberties," Concerned Women for America Web site, September 29, 2005, http://www. cwfa.org/articledisplay.asp?id=9069&department=CFI&categoryid =papers.

Chapter Fourteen   O, Canada!

Evan Wolfson was quoted in Chris Bull, "Northern Enlightenment," *Advocate*, September 17, 2002, p. 23.

Stephen Boisson's story comes to us via his interview with Leanne Burnett Morse, as well as legal documents from his case. The Canadian hate crimes law is Bill C-250 (37th Canadian Parliament, 2nd Session).

Other examples were found in Robert H. Knight and Lindsey Douthit, "Hate Crimes Laws Threaten Religious Liberty," Concerned Women for America Web site, December 12, 2005, http://www.cwfa.org/articledisplay.asp?id=9672&department=C FI&categoryid=papers.

Tristan Emmanuel's quotes are from the TV series *Speechless*, episode three.

The quote from President Barack Obama came from his book, *The Audacity of Hope* (Crown Publishers, NY: Crown Publishers, 2006, p. 222).

References to the Canadian Human Rights Commission were reported in Rory Leishman, "HRCs: Canada's Thought-Police," *Catholic Insight* online magazine, February 1, 2008, p. 9, http://catholicinsight.com/online/editorials/article_780.shtml.

The anecdote about the Anglican bishop in Great Britain came from *Reaney v. Hereford Diocesan Board of Finance*, Case No. 1602844/2006, Employment Tribunal of Cardiff, July 17, 2007, http://www.christian.org.uk/issues/2008/rellib/herefordruling_feb08.pdf.

Reference to "a British couple in Fleetwood . . ." came from "Christians Accused of Homophobia," *BBC News*, December 23, 2005, http://news.bbc.co.uk/1/hi/england/lancashire/4555406.stm.

Reference to "Catholic bishops in Belgium . . ." came from "Belgian Cardinal to be Sued for Remarks on Homosexuality," *EWTNews* online, January 26, 2004, http://www.ewtn.com/vnews/getstory_print.asp?number=43235.

Reference to a British couple who had to give up being foster parents came from Hilary White, "UK Christian Couple Who Refuse to Promote Homosexuality Forced Out of Child Foster Care," *LifeSiteNews* online magazine, October 25, 2007, http://www.lifesitenews.com/ldn/2007/oct/07102502.html.

U.S. Supreme Court Justice Stephen Breyer spoke on international law in an appearance on *This Week with George Stephanopoulos*, ABC News, July 6, 2003. His quote was printed in "Justice: Can Constitution Make It in Global Age?" *WorldNetDaily* online magazine, July 7, 2003, http://www.wnd.com/news/article.asp?ARTICLE_ID=33444.

The ACLU quote came from Ann Beeson and Paul Hoffman, "Introduction," *ACLU International Civil Liberties Report*, ACLU, 2003, http://www.sdshh.com/ICLR/ICLR_2003/1_Introduction.pdf.

Sears and Osten's quote came from Sears and Osten, *The ACLU vs. America: Exposing the Agenda to Redefine Moral Values* (Nashville, TN: B & H Publishing Group, 2005, p. 178).

The French government's laws against homophobia were

reported in John Lichfield, "France to Punish Homophobic and Sexist Remarks with Jail Sentences," *The Independent* (UK), December 9, 2004, p. 27, http://www.independent.co.uk/news/world/europe/france-to-punish-homophobic-and-sexist-remarks-with-jail-sentences-681144.html.

Great Britain's lowering of the age of consent laws was laid out in the Office of Public Sector Information (OPSI), Sexual Offences (Amendment) Act 2000, 2000 Chapter 44, http://www.opsi.gov.uk/ACTS/acts2000/ukpga_20000044_en_1.

Ebba Witt-Brattström's quote originally appeared in Gene Edward Veith, "Doing Without Marriage," by *Worldmag*.com, April 29, 2000, http://www.worldmag.com/articles/3782.

Judge Robert H. Bork's quote was found in Robert H. Bork, *Coercing Virtue: The Worldwide Rule of Judges* (Washington, DC: America Enterprise Institute for Pubic Policy Research Press, 2003).

The reference to a "showdown with religion" came from Sears and Osten, *The ACLU vs. America: Exposing the Agenda to Redefine Moral Values* (Nashville, TN: B & H Publishing Group, 2005, p. 181).

Information on how to get married in Canada came from Lambda Legal, *Traveling to Another State or Country to Marry?* Lambda Legal online brochure, http://www.lambdalegal.org/publications/factsheets/traveling-to-another-state-or-country-to-marry.html.

Chapter Fifteen   The Last Battle

The opening quote from Michael Swift in "Warning to Homophobes," first published in *Gay Community News* in February 1987, is quoted by Ed Vitigliano in "Gay Activists War Against Christianity," *AFA Journal*, February 2006, http://www.afajournal.org/2006/february/206GayWar.asp.

The statistic that thirty percent of Americans favor same-sex marriage came from Knights of Columbus, "Moral Issues and Catholic Values: The California Vote in 2008, Proposition 4," Knights of Columbus survey, Knights of Columbus Web site, October 2008, http://www.kofc.org/un/cmf/resources/proposition4.pdf.

Ira Glasser's quote came from "Civil Liberties at Risk through Ballot Initiatives," ACLU Press Release, November 4, 1998, and was found in Sears and Osten, *The ACLU vs. America: Exposing the Agenda to Redefine Moral Values* (Nashville, TN: B & H Publishing Group, 2005, p. 34), or, if you prefer, the Alliance Defense Fund, "Same-Sex 'Marriage'" Alliance Defense Fund Web site, http://www.alliancedefensefund.org/issues/TraditionalFamily/samesexmarriage.aspx.

The Massachusetts Supreme Judicial Court declaration refers to *Goodridge v. Department of Public Health*, 798 N.E.2d 941 (Mass. 2003).

The California Supreme Court's decision to invalidate the marriage referendum is In re Marriage Cases, 183 P.3d 384 (Cal. 2008), http://www.nclrights.org/site/DocServer/Marriage_Ruling.pdf?docID=3001.

The court's claim that its same-sex marriage decision would "not diminish any other person's constitutional . . ." was quoted from Marc D. Stern, "Will Gay Rights Trample Religious Freedom?" *The Los Angeles Times*, June 17, 2008, http://www.latimes.com/news/opinion/la-oe-stern17-2008jun17,0,5628051.story.

Maggie Gallagher's quote came from personal communication with the author, October 27, 2008.

The New Jersey Supreme Court decision was *Lewis v. Harris*, 908 A.2d 196 (NJ 2006), http://njfamilylaw.foxrothschild.com/tags/lewis-v-harris/.

Scott Hoffman was interviewed by Janet Parshall.

The information about threats against Boston public school

teachers came from Linda Harvey, "Zero Tolerance for Traditional Marriage: It's Legal Now!" *WorldNetDaily* online magazine, October 26, 2004, http://www.worldnetdaily.com/index.php?pageId=27201.

The case of the New Mexico wedding photographer was *Willcock v. Elane Photography*, HRD No. 06-12-20-0685, New Mexico Human Rights Commission, April 9, 2008, http://www.telladf.org/UserDocs/ElaneRuling.pdf.

Sean Kosoky's statement was originally published in David Benkof's editorial, "Why California gays shouldn't celebrate state court ruling," *The Seattle Post-Intelligencer*, May 20, 2008, http://seattlepi.nwsource.com/opinion/363878_califgays21.html.

The source of *The Boston Globe's* comment on Catholic Charities was an unsigned editorial, "Children and the Church," *The Boston Globe*, March 3, 2006, p. A18, http://www.boston.com/news/globe/editorial_opinion/editorials/articles/2006/03/03/children_and_the_church/.

The quote by Philip W. Johnston and Salvatore F. DiMasi was provided by Jonathan Saltzman, "Romney eyes bill exempting religious groups on bias laws," *The Boston Globe*, March 11, 2006, A14, http://www.boston.com/news/local/articles/2006/03/11/romney_eyes_bill_exempting_religious_groups_on_bias_laws/.

The reference "In Canada, an evangelical ministry . . ." was the case *Heintz v. Christian Horizons*, 2008 HRTO 22, Human Rights Tribunal of Ontario, reported in John-Henry Westen, "Huge Christian Ministry to Disabled Fined $23,000 For Rejecting Homosexual Employee," *LifeSiteNews* online magazine, April 25, 2008, http://www.lifesitenews.com/ldn/2008/apr/08042512.html.

The story of Leo "Skip" Childs is taken from Eric Williams, "Truro Man Rejects Bias Label," *Cape Cod Times* online, May 9, 2006. http://www.coalitionformarriage.org/articles/truro-man-rejects-bias-label.aspx.

Matt Staver's quote came from a Liberty Counsel Press Release, "Life, Liberty and Family," June 20, 2005, http://lc.org/pressrelease/2005/nr082205.htm. Matt Staver was also quoted in Allie Martin and Jody Brown, "Inn Owners Sued for Being Hesitant Hosts of 'Civil Union' Reception," *Agape Press News*, July 5, 2005, http://headlines.agapepress.org/archive/7/afa/52005c.asp.

Jonathan Katz's remark was quoted in Dan Savage, "What Does Marriage Mean?" *Salon* online magazine, July 17, 2004, http://dir.salon.com/story/mwt/feature/2004/07/17/gay_marriage/index.html.

The quote from Michelangelo Signorile came from Michelangelo Signorile, "I Do, I Do, I Do, I Do," published in *OUT* magazine, May 1996, and was part of the article by Robert Knight, "'The Sky Is Not Falling'—Yet," Culture and Media Institute Web site, http://www.cultureandmediainstitute.org/articles/2008/20080617152205.aspx.

David L. Chambers's quote came from David Chambers, "What If? The Legal Consequences of Marriage and the Legal Needs of Lesbian and Gay Male Couples," *Michigan Law Review* 95(447, 491), 1996.

The ACLU's position on polygamy can be found on its Web site, http://www.acluutah.org/pluralmarriage.htm.

The Kurtz quote came from Stanley Kurtz, "Beyond Gay Marriage," *The Weekly Standard*, August 4, 2003, p. 26, http://www.weeklystandard.com/Content/Public/Articles/000/000/002/938xpsxy.asp.

A representative of a gay rights organization and openly gay Washington state senator made his statement to journalist David Benkof, "Why California gays shouldn't celebrate state court ruling," *The Seattle Post-Intelligencer*, May 20, 2008, http://seattlepi.nwsource.com/opinion/363878_califgays21.html.

Chapter Sixteen   "Be Angry, but Do Not Sin"

Olivia Turton and her mother Maryann were interviewed by Leanne Burnett Morse for the TV series *Speechless*.

ACKNOWLEDGMENTS

This book is largely based on the TV documentary series of the same name, produced in a partnership of INSP-The Inspiration Network and the American Family Association. The series was created, written, and directed by Executive Producer LeAnne Burnett Morse, who provided outstanding creative leadership. The first fourteen episodes are available on DVD. I hope everyone who reads this book will order and watch this DVD series (and encourage others to do the same)! Those who watch need to understand just how much of the credit for the entire project (the book as well as the series) goes to LeAnne and her colleagues. LeAnne conducted most of the crucial interviews for the show, of which we have made generous use throughout the book. We also frequently have utilized LeAnne's original scripts. There is much in the book for which LeAnne should not be blamed, but a very large portion of "the good stuff," including the original concept and the "story lines" of many of the chapters, is her work. LeAnne also did a final, critical read-through of the manuscript, saving us from some embarrassing errors.

I really am at a loss about what to say about Janet Parshall! She has done such great and brave work for the cause of Christian values over the course of her career. Janet kindly consented to serve as host for the series and made a huge commitment of her valuable time and talent. She did a wonderful job and by helping to make the series such a success also helped make the book possible. Her leadership in the public arena of political and social issues has brought insight and credibility to the project at every level.

LeAnne's colleagues at Inspiration Network have been an integral part of the process of bringing the show from concept to reality. Special thanks go to Ron Shuping, executive vice president of programming, and Doug Butts, vice president of network production, for their tireless leadership and support. The Inspiration Network is part of Inspiration Ministries, a global ministry seeking to impact the world for Christ through media. Chairman and CEO David Cerullo is the visionary leader of this great ministry. Lisa K. Rogers is the senior associate producer for the television show and handled much of the research. Her contributions are great and varied. Kelly Morse developed the title for the show, and, ultimately, the book as well.

Neither the show nor the book would have been possible without the contributions made by our friends at the Alliance Defense Fund, Liberty Legal Institute, Pacific Justice Institute, Liberty Counsel, the Becket Fund, and the Rutherford Institute. The attorneys and staff of these agencies are the "muscle" with which the fight for religious freedom is waged. They are on the front lines every day and they make it possible for those who would be trampled in the culture war to have a voice in the halls of justice.

Also crucial to the effort was AFA staffer, Cherry Sims, who proofed the manuscript and made critical changes.

Ann Coulter amazingly took time out of a frantic schedule, including finishing her own next book (I can't wait to read it),